Foreword

Conflict is a part of everyday life. Unfortunately, many people lack the skills to resolve conflict fairly. Teaching children conflict resolution skills cannot only turn conflict into a positive experience for everyone involved, it can also create a caring school atmosphere, promote problem-solving skills and encourage peace.

The practical activities in *Conflict Resolution* will help children understand how to resolve conflict successfully, and allow them to practise skills and strategies to COMMUNICATE, NEGOTIATE and CONSOLIDATE conflict resolution procedures.

Titles in this series:
    Conflict Resolution – Lower Primary
    Conflict Resolution – Middle Primary
    Conflict Resolution – Upper Primary
    Bullying & Conflict Resolution – Lower Secondary

Contents

Teachers notes

Each student page is supported by a teachers page which provides the following information.

Specific **objectives** explain what the children are expected to demonstrate through completing the activities.

Curriculum Links list the curriculum objectives covered by the activity.

Teacher information provides the teacher with detailed additional information to supplement the student page. Teaching points are also included where appropriate.

On some teacher pages a space has been provided for any **additional notes** the teacher may require, such as reference material or personal information on real-life incidents.

The **drama icon** indicates the inclusion of a drama activity. Drama is an excellent medium for work on conflict resolution.

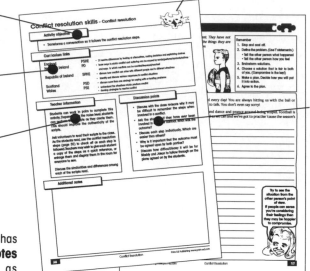

Discussion points have been suggested to further develop ideas on the student page.

An **additional activity** has been included where appropriate.

What is conflict resolution?

Conflict resolution is a process that directs responsibility for solving a conflict to the people involved. Clear steps are followed to achieve a solution that suits both parties. These are:

- defining the **problem**,
- brainstorming **possible solutions**,
- agreeing on the **best solution**,
- putting the best solution into **action**.

In schools, students faced with opposing viewpoints will often go to a teacher to sort out a conflict and decide on a solution. Instead, students should be encouraged to use conflict resolution to resolve minor conflicts such as name-calling, rumours, taking property without asking, teasing and invading personal space. The conflict resolution process teaches students that conflict need not be a negative experience, but can motivate change and provide opportunities.

This book helps students to understand conflict resolution steps, comprehend, analyse and solve conflict resolution scenarios, gain an understanding of the consequences of actions during conflict, explore conflict in history, and use role-play to problem-solve and identify feelings during conflict.

What is peer mediation?

Peer mediation is used when conflicting parties have tried to solve a conflict on their own but cannot agree on a fair solution. A neutral third student is then asked to help.

Peer mediation should only be attempted in a school where staff and students have attended a training course. As not all students have the personality to be effective mediators, students who are to be trained in the process should be chosen carefully.

Peer mediators are trained to:
- use conflict resolution steps to help two people solve a problem,
- listen to both sides of the story,
- use a consistent approach to solving problems,
- be impartial,
- attack the problem, rather than the people involved,
- encourage the conflicting parties to treat each other with respect.

This book helps students to understand and use mediation steps, how to use compromise, understand where mediation should take place and evaluate mediation situations in which they have been involved.

Peer mediation is still in its infancy in terms of widespread practice in the UK and Ireland, but it is popular in the USA and Australia.

CONFLICT RESOLUTION

0583C–09/03

Conflict Resolution—Upper Primary
Prim-Ed Publishing

Published in 2003 by R.I.C. Publications
Reprinted under license in 2003 by Prim-Ed Publishing

ISBN 1 86400 780 X
PR–0583

Additional titles available in this series:
Conflict Resolution—Lower Primary
Conflict Resolution—Middle Primary
Bullying and Conflict Resolution—Secondary
Conflict Resolution Posters

Prim-Ed Publishing Pty Ltd

Home Page: http://www.prim-ed.com
Email: sales@prim-ed.com

Teachers notes

What is negotiation?

Negotiation is the problem-solving process used to resolve conflict. The goal of negotiation is to create a solution the conflicting parties agree to.

Before a negotiation meeting, the people involved should think carefully about what they will say. The parties then meet in a quiet, neutral place; e.g. a 'negotiating table' in a corner of the classroom. The conflict is identified and an agreement to resolve it is made.

An important part of the negotiation process is using 'I' statements to describe wants and needs. When describing wants and needs, students should speak calmly and give reasons. When listening to someone else, they should demonstrate active listening through positive feedback and eye contact.

Effective negotiation relies on clear communication, problem-solving skills, showing respect and a focus on finding a 'win-win' solution.

Focus on the problem, not the person.

This book helps students to understand the steps that should be used during negotiation, express their needs and wants, understand what makes a good negotiator and write a negotiating play script.

What skills and attitudes should be fostered?

For conflict resolution to be effective in a class or school, certain skills and attitudes are necessary. The following skills and attitudes are a focus of the activities in this book.

• Empathy and tolerance

Conflict is often caused by a lack of understanding of others. Empathy and tolerance should therefore be encouraged in students. Activities that require students to put themselves in someone else's place and imagine how they feel can help to foster empathy. Tolerance is an on-going process that teaches children not to hate. Teachers can teach tolerance most effectively by modelling tolerant behaviour in the classroom and playground, ensuring students are exposed to multicultural literature and images, and teaching them about various faiths, ethnicities and lifestyles. Educating students to be tolerant will:

- promote the understanding and acceptance of individual differences,
- promote the idea that differences can enhance our relationships and enrich our society,
- minimise generalisations and stereotyping,
- promote the need to combat prejudice and discrimination.

Students will learn about empathy and tolerance in this book through activities that help them recognise prejudice and understand other students in their class.

A core belief creates blindspots so it's important to really hear the other person's story.

Teachers notes

• Communication skills

Speaking and listening skills are vital to prevent and resolve conflicts. Students should be encouraged to speak clearly and calmly and use eye contact, particularly when involved in negotiation. The role-play activities in this book provide students with opportunities to practise these skills. Active listening also needs to be learnt and practised because people involved in conflict often fail to interpret correctly what others are saying.

Students will explore the value of good communication in this book through activities that help them to recognise a good listener, understand passive, assertive and aggressive communication and use 'I' statements correctly.

Communication is an expression of thought. Barriers such as anger can lead to that communication not being received. It's hard to accept anything from someone when angry. It is important to cushion a person's emotions when negotiating a solution.

• Teamwork

The ability to work with others towards a common goal is a vital conflict resolution skill that can be practised in a range of curriculum areas. The following qualities are necessary for a team to function at its best:

- working towards a clear goal – the team clearly understands and works towards the goal that is to be achieved.

- good communication – the team members listen to each other with respect and willingly share their ideas without domination.

- consideration – the team members encourage and support each other's ideas, giving critical feedback.

Students will learn about teamwork in this book through activities that allow them to participate in team-building, evaluate their teamwork and discover the qualities of a good team.

• Problem-solving

Students should become familiar with problem-solving steps to solve conflict. The following steps should be taught:

- define the problem,

- brainstorm possible solutions,

- evaluate the ideas,

- decide on a solution and carry it out.

Students will explore problem-solving in this book through activities that require them to use the steps described above.

• Anger management

It is important for teachers to create an atmosphere in their classrooms that allows students to express and manage angry feelings. This can be done by ensuring that all rules are clear, fair and consistent, adopting anger management strategies for certain students, and modelling positive anger management strategies such as taking a deep breath, getting away from the situation that is causing the anger, trying to relax, or self-talk.

Students will learn about anger management in this book through activities that help them to recognise suitable and unsuitable reactions to conflict.

• Peacemaking

The goal of peacemaking is to ensure that all people are able to fully enjoy their human rights. For students to be effective peace makers, they should have an understanding of what peace is, its importance and how they can create it. To begin with, they should understand that peace is not a passive state (a lack of war), but a process which relies on communication and action to be created and sustained. Teachers should emphasise resolving conflicts at all levels to reach a peaceful solution where everyone wins.

Students will learn about the value of peace in this book through activities that help them to reflect on what peace means and by finding peaceful solutions to situations.

Teachers notes

How can conflict resolution be implemented in a classroom or school?

Schools that have implemented conflict resolution programmes report that conflicts are being handled more quickly, physical fighting is declining and more caring behaviour is shown.

The first step in implementing conflict resolution programmes is to create a cooperative classroom and school environment where rules, rights and responsibilities are clearly stated, and where students feel able to say what they feel. The school should also hold the belief that social skills are as important as academic skills.

Teachers can also:

- teach or encourage the skills and attitudes covered in 'What skills and attitudes should be fostered?'

- inform parents of conflict resolution steps. Ask them to support the programme by encouraging their children to use conflict resolution steps to solve problems at home,

- introduce mediation training courses for students and staff (Details of mediation courses can be found on the Internet. Try typing 'school mediation courses' into a search engine.),

- teach students how to deliver 'I' statements correctly,

- hang charts with conflict resolution steps in the classroom and around the school,

- create a 'negotiating corner' in the classroom.

Curriculum Links

Country	Year/Group	Subject	Curriculum Strand	Content Objectives
England	KS2 (Y5/6)	PSHE and Citizenship	2a	• research, discuss and debate problems and events
			2c	• realise the consequences of anti-social and aggressive behaviours, such as bullying and racism
			2d	• know there are different kinds of responsibilities and rights at home/school/community, and that these can sometimes conflict with each other
			2e	• reflect on moral, social and cultural issues, using imagination to understand other people's experiences
			2f	• resolve differences by looking at alternatives, making decisions and explaining choices
			4a	• know that their actions affect themselves and others, to care about other people's feelings and to try to see things from their points of view
			4c	• develop skills to be effective in relationships
			4d	• realise the nature and consequences of racism, teasing, bullying and aggressive behaviours, and how to respond to them and ask for help
			4e	• recognise and challenge stereotypes
			4f	• know that similarities and differences between people arise from a number of factors
			4g	• know where individuals can get help and support
Northern Ireland*	KS 2 (Y6/7)	Personal Development	Personal Understanding and Health	• investigate their personal self image, self-esteem and feelings and emotions
			Mutual Understanding in the Local and Wider Community	• know how to recognise, manage and express their feelings and emotions • recognise and be sensitive to the feelings of others • know when it is important to express their feelings to others and how to do this in a positive way • investigate situations they and others have faced and how this made them feel • recognise bullying, its effects and how it might feel to be in someone else's shoes • recognise real friendship, how to respond to bullying and how to support peers in a positive way • know ways in which conflict and suffering can be caused by words/gestures/symbols/actions and ways in which conflicts can be avoided/lessened/resolved • know how to be confident and express their views in unfamiliar circumstances • realise the consequences of anti-social behaviour
Republic of Ireland	5th/6th Class	SPHE	Myself	• recognise and appreciate that each person is a unique individual • acquire ability and confidence to identify, discuss and explore a range of feelings • discuss and practise how to express and cope with various feelings in an appropriate manner • recognise that decisions have consequences • discuss and practise a simple decision-making strategy • identify sources of help in solving problems
			Myself and Others	• discuss and identify behaviour that is important for harmony in family life • explore the importance of friendship and interacting with others • consider problems that can arise in friendships and other relationships and how these could be handled • explore how the opinions, views or expectations of others can influence how people relate to each other • practise and recognise the importance of care, consideration, courtesy and good manners when dealing with others • recognise, discuss and understand bullying and its effects • explore and discuss how individuals can deal with being bullied, knowing that others are being bullied and being a bully • explore and practise the many verbal and non-verbal ways in which people communicate with each other

Curriculum Links

Country	Year/Group	Subject	Curriculum Strand	Content Objectives
Republic of Ireland cont.			Myself and Others cont.	• listen actively to others and respect what each person has to say • examine the various ways in which language can be used to isolate and discriminate against people • appreciate the importance of maintaining a personal stance while also respecting the beliefs, values and opinions of others • discuss how conflict can arise with different people and in different situations • identify and discuss various responses to conflict situations • explore and practise how to handle conflict without being aggressive
			Myself and Wider World	• practise ways of working together • explore how justice and peace can be promoted between people and groups
Scotland	P5–7	Personal and Social Development	Self-Awareness	• begin to recognise a range of emotions and how they deal with them
			Self-Esteem	• be positive about themselves and their social and cultural backgrounds • approach difficulties with confidence • recognise their perception of self is affected by responses from others
			Inter-Personal Relationships	• adopt different roles within groups • demonstrate respect and tolerance towards others
			Independence and Inter-dependence	• discuss more than one strategy for coping with or tackling problems • take increasing responsibility for their own actions
		Health	Emotional (D)	• demonstrate an understanding of their emotional needs and strengths • recognise ways behaviour can influence people's relationships
			Emotional (E)	• demonstrate responsible strategies to deal with a range of situations and emotions in relationships • show ways in which they can seek help and advice
			Emotional (F)	• demonstrate personal and interpersonal skills
			Social (D)	• recognise issues of discrimination and the right to equal opportunity for all members of the community
Wales	KS2 (Y5/6)	PSE	Attitudes and Values	• show care and consideration for others and be sensitive towards their feelings • respect others and value uniqueness • value friends/families as a source of love/support • value and celebrate cultural difference and diversity • take increasing responsibility for their actions • feel positive about themselves and confident in their own values
			Skills	• listen carefully/question/respond to others • empathise with others' experiences and feelings • make and maintain friendships • develop strategies to resolve conflict and deal with bullying • develop decision-making skills • work cooperatively to tackle problems
			Knowledge and Understanding	• understand the benefits of friends and families and the challenges and issues that can arise • understand the nature of bullying and harm that can result • know and understand the range of their own and others' feelings and emotions • understand the situations which produce conflict • recognise uniqueness of individuals • understand that their actions have consequences

*The curriculum guidelines for Northern Ireland have been taken from the proposals for the revised primary curriculum (April 2002). At the time of going to print, the finalised curriculum was not available.

Peer mediation agreement form

Date of mediation _____

Place of mediation _____

Children involved in conflict _____

_____

Mediator _____

Description of conflict _____

_____

_____

_____

_____

Solution agreed to _____

_____

_____

_____

_____

_____

_____

_____

Agreement sealed by: a handshake ☐   other ☐ _____

I agree to this solution.

signed _____ date _____

I agree to this solution.

signed _____ date _____

Mediator's signature

signed _____ date _____

Glossary

Below are some specialised conflict resolution terms and related vocabulary used in this book. It is suggested that the meanings of these terms are consciously taught to the children to gain maximum benefit from this conflict resolution programme.

aggressive
An aggressive person acts as though their rights are more important than others. They seek to get their own way as often as possible.

assertive
An assertive person respects others and themselves equally. They feel comfortable enough to stand up for themselves and express their opinions, while still considering the needs of others.

compromise
A compromise is the settling of a problem or argument by both sides agreeing to give way a little from what each really wants.

conflict
A conflict situation may be caused by an event or a difference in two or more people's ideas/opinions. This causes unhappiness and disagreement.

empathy
To feel sympathetic towards another person.

'I' statements
'I' statements tell the way someone feels about a situation, using the word 'I' at the beginning of the statement; e.g. 'I don't like it when you call me names', 'I feel angry when you are always late.' 'I' statements should be used in the negotiation stage of conflict resolution. They are preferable to a person beginning a sentence with 'You ...' because this implicitly accuses the other person of causing the problem and decreases the chance of resolution. ('I' statements are also called "'I' messages" in some schools and publications.)

lose-lose
A conflict resolution result in which neither person achieves his or her wants and needs.

mediation
A process where a neutral third party listens to all sides to try and resolve a conflict.

mediator
A neutral third party who is called in to help two people in conflict solve the problem themselves.

negative feeling
A negative feeling is a 'bad' feeling, when a person feels unhappy.

negotiate
When people work or talk together to try to achieve an agreement to end conflict.

negotiating table
A quiet area set aside for students to solve conflict.

positive feeling
A positive feeling is a 'good' feeling, when a person feels happy.

passive
A passive person acts as though the rights of others are more important than their own. They may not feel confident enough to say how they feel.

prejudice
When people judge another by what they see or hear about a person, rather than what the person is really like.

tolerance
A tolerant person tries to understand and appreciate difference. Tolerance is a skill which can reduce conflict.

win-lose
A conflict resolution result in which one person achieves his or her wants and needs but the other person does not.

win-win
A conflict resolution result in which both people at least partially achieve their wants and needs.

Note: several other conflict resolution terms are used in the teachers notes. It is suggested that, at the teacher's discretion, these words could be used in discussion, to expand children's vocabulary. These words include:

discrimination	gender
impartial	justice
multicultural	physical reaction
retaliation	stereotype
verbal reaction	

Understanding conflict – What is conflict?

Activity objectives

- Understands the meaning of conflict.
- Understands how people react to conflict.

Curriculum links

England	PSHE	• 2f resolve differences by looking at alternatives, making decisions and explaining choices
Northern Ireland	PD	• know ways in which conflict and suffering can be caused by words/gestures/symbols/actions and ways in which conflicts can be avoided/lessened/resolved
Republic of Ireland	SPHE	• discuss how conflict can arise with different people and in different situations
		• identify and discuss various responses to conflict situations
Scotland	PSD	• discuss more than one strategy for coping with or tackling problems
Wales	PSE	• understand the situations which produce conflict
		• develop strategies to resolve conflict

Teacher information

Conflict among individuals and groups is a part of everyday life. Causes of conflict include limited resources, different needs, values or beliefs, and prejudice. Common justifications people give for becoming involved in conflict include justice, retaliation, defence or maintaining an image.

In this activity, the conflict is a dispute between two neighbours, both of whom are unwilling to compromise. Students are asked to define the conflict, the feelings of the people involved and their impression of what is happening/what should be happening.

Discussion points

- What are some common causes of conflict?
- How can conflict be a positive experience?
- What feelings do people involved in conflict usually experience?
- Is there more than one good way to solve a conflict?
- Discuss some major national or international conflicts occuring in the news and their basic causes; e.g. limited resources, different values, oppression etc.

Additional notes

① Read the newspaper article below.

DING-DONG DILEMMA

How annoying do you find the sound of a doorbell? For Tony Bramston, it is pure torture.

Three months ago, Mr Bramston's neighbour, Janine Garwood, installed a doorbell that plays a variety of nursery rhymes whenever it is pressed. And that's often.

'Mrs Garwood runs a childminding business from home, so there are at least 12 people arriving every morning and afternoon,' says Mr Bramston. 'I can hear the doorbell from every room in my house. I am a shiftworker and I need to sleep during the day, but it is impossible.'

Mrs Garwood says she does not want to get rid of her unique doorbell. 'I paid a lot of money for it, and it's good for business—the bright and cheerful sound is appealing to children. Besides, I have every right to own a doorbell.'

Mr Bramston first approached Mrs Garwood about the problem one week after the doorbell was installed. He admits he probably offended Mrs Garwood by saying the doorbell was 'noise pollution'. Mrs Garwood says that she reacted by calling Mr Bramston insulting names.

'Both of us have bad tempers,' said Mr Bramston. 'The meeting ended with us screaming angry words at each other.'

Mr Bramston and Mrs Garwood agree the conflict needs to be resolved, but at this stage neither has any intention of backing down.

② Describe the conflict in this article and how both people are involved.

_____

_____

_____

③ Write the feelings and emotions of both neighbours. Circle any they have in common.

Mr Bramston

Mrs Garwood

④ Write your opinion of how the neighbours are dealing with the conflict. Give reasons.

_____

_____

_____

_____

_____

⑤ What do you think should be done to resolve the conflict? Try to think of a fair solution.

_____

_____

_____

_____

_____

Understanding conflict – What escalates conflict?

Curriculum links

England	PSHE	• 2f resolve differences by looking at alternatives, making decisions and explaining choices
Northern Ireland	PD	• know ways in which conflict and suffering can be caused by words/gestures/symbols/actions and ways in which conflicts can be avoided/lessened/resolved
Republic of Ireland	SPHE	• discuss how conflict can arise with different people and in different situations
		• identify and discuss various responses to conflict situations
Scotland	PSD	• discuss more than one strategy for coping with or tackling problems
Wales	PSE	• understand the situations which produce conflict
		• develop strategies to resolve conflict

Teacher information

Most people associate conflict with negative thoughts or feelings such as unhappiness, anger and violence, but if dealt with correctly, conflict can also be a positive experience, motivating change and providing opportunities.

Our families, cultures, schools, workplaces and communities teach us different ways to deal with conflict, but it is commonly accepted that one side wins and the other loses. However, students should be encouraged to strive for a 'win-win' outcome to conflict. This concept is covered in the pages concerned with conflict resolution.

People involved in conflict often escalate negative emotions verbally (e.g. teasing, name-calling, swearing), or physically (e.g. shoving, hitting, stamping feet). In this activity, students reflect on the behaviour of two people involved in a conflict and consider how they could change their behaviour to make the experience a positive one. Positive outcomes they might consider if Jack and Tim had behaved differently could include playing chess together, agreeing to share the chess set, becoming friends and so on.

Discussion points

- What kinds of things can people say to escalate conflict? What kinds of things can they do? Which type of behaviour is worse?
- Why should we try to avoid escalating conflict?
- What are some things we can do to stop conflict escalating?
- How can conflict be a positive experience?

Additional notes

What escalates conflict?

Most people think of conflict as a negative experience. But conflict can bring about change or new opportunities—if it is dealt with properly. Unfortunately, people involved in conflict often do things that escalate it, or heighten the negative emotions of the people involved. This can be done verbally (e.g. name-calling or teasing) or physically (e.g. pushing, kicking).

Imagine that Tim, a younger child at your school, tells you the following:

'Yesterday, the teacher said we could play games for half an hour. Jack and I both got to the chess set at the same time. I asked him politely if I could use it. He said no, called me a horrible name and wrestled the box from me. I felt angry. I yelled at him and snatched it out of his hands. We then had a tug of war with the game. Jack managed to get it away from me. As he walked away, he said I was weak. I picked up some counters and threw them at him.'

① Circle all the physical reactions to the conflict in blue and all the verbal reactions in red.

② Tim asks you these questions. Answer them as helpfully as you can.

(a) *'Things really got out of control! What did we do wrong?'*

_____

_____

_____

_____

(b) *'I think Jack behaved worse than I did because he called me names. What do you think?'*

_____

_____

_____

_____

(c) *'What do you think I should have done differently? What should Jack have done differently? What difference would it have made?'*

_____

_____

_____

_____

_____

Understanding conflict - Prejudice

Activity objective

- Gains an understanding of prejudice and making assumptions.

Curriculum links

England	PSHE	• 4e recognise and challenge stereotypes
Northern Ireland	PD	• demonstrate respect and tolerance towards others
Republic of Ireland	SPHE	• explore how the opinions, views or expectations of others can influence how people relate to each other
Scotland	Health	• recognise issues of discrimination
Wales	PSE	• respect others and value uniqueness

Teacher information

Prejudice—making assumptions about people based on how they look or what others say—is a major cause of conflict. People are often attacked physically and/or verbally as a result of a lack of understanding by others.

It is common to base initial judgments of people on stereotypes. Stereotypes depend on conventional ideas about groups of people which may include attitudes, interests, characteristic traits or physical features.

We all stereotype people to some extent. However, stereotyping can lead to discrimination and intolerance.

After students report to the class in this activity, teachers should lead a class discussion about what the students learnt from the activity.

Discussion points

- What is a stereotype?
- What is prejudice?
- Why should we avoid stereotyping others?
- Discuss examples of how prejudice against others can lead to conflict.

Additional notes

Prejudice

Sometimes, conflict results when one person is prejudiced against another—that is, he/she has assumptions about what the person is like simply because of what he/she sees or has been told.

1 Write the assumptions someone might make about these people at first sight.

_____

_____

_____

_____

_____

_____

_____

_____

_____

_____

_____

_____

_____

_____

_____

_____

_____

Can YOU see past the exterior?

2 Find a group of four people and discuss your answers to Question 1, ticking any similarities you find. Then consider these questions.

- *Why do you think there were similarities among your answers?*
- *What is the problem with making assumptions about people based on how they look?*
- *How do you think prejudice might cause conflict?*

3 Report your answers to the class.

Communications and feelings – Identifying feelings

Activity objectives

- Shows an understanding of how people feel during conflict.
- Identifies how people show feelings through words and actions.

Curriculum links

England	PSHE	• 4a care about other people's feelings and to try to see things from their points of view
Northern Ireland	PD	• recognise, manage and express feelings and be sensitive to feelings of others
Republic of Ireland	SPHE	• acquire ability and confidence to identify, discuss and explore a range of feelings
Scotland	PSD	• recognise a range of emotions and how they deal with them
Wales	PSE	• empathise with others' experiences and feelings

Teacher information

Students should be able to identify common feelings of people involved in conflict. These may include positive and negative feelings; e.g. anger, disappointment, fear, frustration, confidence, calmness.

Before completing the activity, students should have an understanding of the terms 'win-win', 'win-lose' and 'lose-lose' (see glossary pxi and the Negotiation activities on pages 42 to 53).

Ask the students to find partners to work with, then distribute one copy of the role-plays below to each pair.

Encourage the students to use well-structured arguments in their role-plays, as well as gesture, facial expression and vocal expression to indicate their characters' feelings.

Students may perform for the whole class or a small group.

Teachers may like to hold a class discussion about the feelings of people in conflict after the presentations.

Discussion points

- What are some common feelings people involved in conflict have?
- How do they show these feelings?
- Which is the fairest type of outcome to a conflict? Why?

THE DIARY

A and B are good friends.

A walks into a room and catches B reading his/her diary. A has never let anyone read the diary—it is private. B has just read some comments about him/her that he/she does not like.

Role-play the conflict that occurs after A walks into the room.

THE BENCH

A is new to B's school.

B walks out of his/her classroom at lunchtime to find A sitting on the bench where B and his/her gang always sit. B rudely tells A to move.

Role-play the conflict that occurs when A refuses B's command.

Identifying feelings

① Read each scenario carefully, then complete the following tasks with your partner.

(a) Decide who will play A and B in each scenario.

(b) Write three possible endings for each scenario using the headings below; e.g. 'A pushes B and then runs away'. Add words to describe how you think A and B would feel about each ending to the conflict, considering how fair the outcome is.

· a win-win ending (both characters are happy with the outcome – may need compromise)

❑ The Diary

Feelings: A

          B

❑ The Bench

Feelings: A

          B

· a win-lose ending (only one character gets what he/she wants)

❑ The Diary

Feelings: A

          B

❑ The Bench

Feelings: A

          B

· a lose-lose ending (neither character likes the outcome)

❑ The Diary

Feelings: A

          B

❑ The Bench

Feelings: A

          B

(c) Choose one 'win-win' ending, one 'win-lose' ending and one 'lose-lose' ending to act out. Tick the three you choose.

② Practise your three role-plays. Make sure you say at least five lines each.

> **Choose your words and actions carefully to show how your character is feeling.**

③ Perform your role-plays for the class or a small group.

④ Choose one of the role-plays you performed. Describe how you used words and actions to show your character's feelings.

Communications and feelings – How would you feel?

Activity objectives

- Understands how people express feelings in conflict situations.
- Considers how some conflict situations might make him/her feel.
- Reflects on how he/she expresses some feelings.

Curriculum links

England	PSHE	• 4a care about other people's feelings and to try to see things from their points of view
Northern Ireland	PD	• recognise, manage and express feelings and be sensitive to feelings of others
Republic of Ireland	SPHE	• acquire ability and confidence to identify, discuss and explore a range of feelings
Scotland	PSD	• recognise a range of emotions and how they deal with them
Wales	PSE	• empathise with others' experiences and feelings

Teacher information

After the activity is completed, teachers may like to hold a class discussion about appropriate and inappropriate ways to express feelings.

Discussion points

- What is a common way to express anger/fear/frustration/sadness/happiness and so on?
- What effect can feelings have on a conflict?

Additional notes

How would you feel?

1. Read the stories below. List the feelings of Steven and Isobel and describe how they expressed these feelings. Give your opinion on their reactions.

> *Steven's younger sister Jade won't stop hanging around him and his friends. Steven roughly tells her to go away. Jade responds by poking out her tongue and threatening to tell their mother that Steven is being mean. Jade refuses to leave and keeps hanging around, even though Steven continues making rude comments about her.*

Steven's feelings _____

_____

How expressed _____

_____

Opinion _____

Isobel's feelings _____

_____

How expressed _____

_____

Opinion _____

_____

> *Isobel and her friends leave their art project in the classroom at lunchtime. They return just in time to see Adam and his friends knock it to the ground, damaging it. Adam's group don't notice until Isobel shows them what has happened. They say it is not their fault—the girls shouldn't have left it alone. Isobel reacts by threatening to damage Adam's group's project. Both groups begin shouting at each other. Adam eventually suggests to Isobel that his group will help to fix her group's project. Isobel agrees.*

2. Read the beginning of each of the stories again. Consider how you would feel, and how you would express this. Discuss your answers with a partner.

Put yourself in the place of Jade and Adam.

Jade's situation

My feelings

How I would express them _____

_____

_____

_____

_____

Adam's situation

My feelings

How I would express them _____

_____

_____

_____

_____

Communication and feelings – Responses to conflict

Activity objective

- Evaluates how he/she responds to conflict.

Curriculum links

England	PSHE	• 2f resolve differences by looking at alternatives, making decisions and explaining choices
Northern Ireland	PD	• know ways in which conflict and suffering can be caused by words/gestures/symbols/actions and ways in which conflicts can be avoided/lessened/resolved
Republic of Ireland	SPHE	• discuss how conflict can arise with different people and in different situations
		• identify and discuss various responses to conflict situations
Scotland	PSD	• discuss more than one strategy for coping with or tackling problems
Wales	PSE	• understand the situations which produce conflict
		• develop strategies to resolve conflict

Teacher information

The following page can be completed as a class exercise or given to individual students after a conflict has taken place.

Discussion points

- Do you think you respond well to conflict?
- What could you improve about your typical response to conflict?
- What did you learn from the last conflict you were involved in?

Additional notes

Responses to conflict

How do you usually respond to conflict? Answer the questions below.

1 What type of conflict were you last involved in? _____

2 Who else was involved? _____

3 Tick the box or boxes that describe what you did.

> To handle yourself, use your head.
> To handle others, use your heart.

(a) *When the conflict began:*

I ignored it. ☐

I confronted the situation after waiting for a while. ☐

I confronted the situation immediately. ☐

Other _____

_____

(b) *During the conflict:*

I reacted with violent words or actions. ☐

Describe _____

_____

I reacted nonviolently. ☐

Describe _____

_____

4 Tick the box or boxes that show the result of the conflict.

People were hurt. ☐	*We agreed to disagree.* ☐
Describe	*Describe*
We used negotiation. ☐	*We used mediation.* ☐
Describe	*Describe*

Communication and feelings – Being a good listener

Activity objective

- Identifies the steps to becoming an active listener.

Curriculum links

England	PSHE	• 4c develop skills to be effective in relationships
Northern Ireland	PD	• know ways in which conflict can be caused and ways in which conflicts can be avoided
Republic of Ireland	SPHE	• listen actively to others and respect what each person has to say
Scotland	Health	• demonstrate personal and interpersonal skills
Wales	PSE	• listen carefully/question/respond to others

Teacher information

Ask the students to think about any conflicts they have been involved in over the past month. What was the cause of the problem? Some students may state that the cause of the problem was a misunderstanding or miscommunication—the other person 'didn't listen'.

Listening is an important skill that needs to be learnt and practised. Many people only 'half' listen as they are thinking about what they might say when the speaker stops. Some people don't wait for the speaker to stop and interrupt him or her in the middle of a sentence.

Discussion points

- Why is it important to be a good listener?
- What can happen when you don't listen to someone properly?

Additional activity

Give each student a blank sheet of art paper. Find a picture of a detailed scene and describe it to the class. Be specific; for example, 'The dog is on the left of the tree and in front of the bush'. Continue giving instructions. When the students have completed their art, show them the original drawing. Compare their drawings to yours. Did they listen carefully?

How to be a good listener

- *Look at the speaker.*

- *Listen without interrupting.*

- *Do not offer advice or give suggestions unless asked.*

- *Ask questions to find out more.*

- *Show that you understand by nodding, making eye contact and using facial expressions.*

- *Repeat what you have heard in your own words (paraphrase).*

Conflict Resolution
Prim-Ed Publishing www.prim-ed.com

Being a good listener

1 Have you ever heard someone say (or said yourself), 'You hear me but you never listen to me!'? What do you think is the difference between **hearing** and **listening**?

_____

_____

_____

_____

2 Is there someone you share your ideas, thoughts and feelings with? Is that person a good listener? What do you think makes a person a good listener? List your ideas.

_____

_____

_____

_____

Don't interrupt with a story of your own.

One quality of being a good listener is being able to paraphrase (repeat what someone has said using different words). Good listeners do this to show the speaker that they understand what he or she is saying. (They don't give their opinions unless they are asked.)

3 Read the passage below and give examples of how you could paraphrase each statement. The first one has been done for you.

(a) *A friend comes and sits down next to you during lunch looking agitated. She tells you that she has just had a disagreement with her brother.*

'He's a buffoon! He always assumes that because I'm the youngest I have to do what he says!'

'You're upset because he tells you what to do.'

(b) *'He told me I have to take his basketball gear home with me because he is going to a friend's place after school. Now I have to carry two bags home!'*

_____

(c) *'Not only that, he wants me to tell Mum and Dad that he is at John's house when he is actually going to Brodie's! He knows I hate lying!'*

_____

(d) *'I am so angry with him but I just go along with everything he says!'*

_____

4 Being a good listener also means offering your advice and suggestions **when they are asked for**. What would be your advice for 'your friend' having a conflict with her brother?

_____

_____

_____

_____

5 Do you consider yourself to be a good listener? ⊂ **Yes** ⊂ **No** ⊂ (If you are not sure, ask a friend.)

Communication and feelings - Communication

Activity objectives

- Identifies different styles of communication.
- Identifies how he/she communicates.

Curriculum links

England	PSHE	• 4c develop skills to be effective in relationships
Northern Ireland	PD	• know how to be confident and express their views in unfamiliar circumstances
Republic of Ireland	SPHE	• explore and practise how to handle conflict without being aggressive
Scotland	Health	• demonstrate personal and interpersonal skills
Wales	PSE	• listen carefully/question/respond to others

Teacher information

The three styles of communication are passive, aggressive and assertive.

Passive people act as though the rights of others are more important than theirs. They may do something they don't want to do and have an inability to express how they feel.

Aggressive people act as though their rights are more important than others. They try to get their own way through bullying or physical violence.

Assertive people respect others and themselves equally. They stand up for themselves and say what they think without hurting others.

Discussion points

- Discuss what kind of attributes assertive, passive and aggressive people may have.
- Can a person be passive and assertive, depending on the situation? Think about the student who is quiet at school but very assertive when surrounded by younger siblings at home. Another student may be very assertive and aggressive on the sports field but passive in the classroom.
- Explain that it is possible for people to practise changing the way they speak ('I' statements) and act (body language); training themselves to be more assertive or less aggressive.
- Show a range of pictures. Discuss whether the person feels good or bad about himself/herself. Students can role-play how they look, act and speak when they are feeling good or bad about themselves.

Styles of communication

Passive

Aggressive

Assertive

Conflict Resolution

Prim-Ed Publishing www.prim-ed.com

Communication

There are three main ways to communicate – passively, assertively or aggressively.

1 Circle the response that you think is most similar to what your own would be.

(i) 'Move! That's my chair!'
- (a) 'OK ... I'm sorry.' *(passive)*
- (b) 'I was sitting here first. Please find another chair.' *(assertive)*
- (c) 'Get real! You can go and get your own chair!' *(aggressive)*

(ii) 'Go and knock over that bin!'
- (a) 'Umm ... but I'll get into trouble .... OK, all right.' *(passive)*
- (b) 'I don't want to do that. It's not right.' *(assertive)*
- (c) 'You knock over the bin yourself!' *(aggressive)*

(iii) 'You are always taking my things without asking. You're such a thief!'
- (a) 'I know, I'm sorry. I won't do it again ... sorry.' *(passive)*
- (b) 'I feel upset when you accuse me of taking your things without asking because I always ask first.' *(assertive)*
- (c) 'I'm not a thief! You're a liar!' *(aggressive)*

Anger is only one letter short of danger.

2 Now that you have read the examples, write a sentence describing each style of communication.

passive _____

assertive _____

aggressive _____

3 What style of communicator do you think you are?   passive/assertive/aggressive

(a) Ask two friends. Do they agree?   Friend 1 [Yes] [No]   Friend 2 [Yes] [No]

(b) Give an example that shows the type of communicator you are.

_____

_____

_____

4 In pairs, write a short script on the back of this sheet between two people. Decide what type of communicator each person will be first.

(a) Role-play the discussion and ask another group to try to guess what type of communicator each person is. Here are your choices:

• passive + passive	• passive + assertive
• assertive + assertive	• assertive + aggressive
• aggressive + aggressive	• passive + aggressive

(b) Role-play the discussion again but choose a different style of communication for one or both of the people. You will need to change the dialogue to meet the style of communication.

Communication and feelings

Activity objective

- Communicates by participating in drama activities.

Curriculum links

England	PSHE	• 4c develop skills to be effective in relationships
Northern Ireland	PD	• know how to be confident and express their views in unfamiliar circumstances
Republic of Ireland	SPHE	• explore and practise verbal and non-verbal ways in which people communicate with each other
Scotland	Health	• demonstrate personal and interpersonal skills
Wales	PSE	• listen carefully/question/respond to others

Teacher information

Being able to communicate effectively enables students to feel that they are getting their point across.

Communication may take many forms. The same point of view or opinion may be expressed in a number of creative ways. Students may feel more confident to express their feelings through poetry, artwork, drama, mime or creative writing.

Games such as 'Shapes' and 'Sculptures', where students form groups of three to create a shape as directed by the teacher use body language to communicate ideas. Activities such as debates, short talks, role-plays, singing, reciting raps or poetry, allowing students to lead displays or assembly items, or assisting younger children are only a few ways to develop confidence and communication skills. Most students have talents in one or two particular areas and would prefer to communicate using these methods. It is advisable to give the students opportunities to develop and experience skills and activities in a variety of communication methods.

The activities on page 19 allow the students to use a variety of creative methods to communicate the same thoughts.

Discussion points

- What is your most commonly used method of communication?
- If you want to share your thoughts or feelings with someone, who would you choose and how would you do it?
- Which 'creative' method of communication do you enjoy using the most?
- Think of a painting or play that you have seen. What do you think the artist or playwright is trying to express?
- Which creative method of communication did most people choose?
- Were there any class members who displayed a talent that you didn't know they had?

Additional notes

Communication activities

• One-word scenes

In pairs, students create scenes with each line being only one word.

For example:
Hi
Hello
Dance?
OK
Own!
What?

Lots of expression and body language must be used to get the message across. Teachers can offer some ideas for scenes or starting lines. This is not the easiest activity in the world, and students will need some help to get started.

• Five-minute plays

Teachers allocate a concept to small groups of students; for example, fear, loneliness, sorrow, hiding etc. Groups have five minutes to rehearse a scene which shows this. Good communication is needed to show the concept as well as to decide on what to do in such a short time.

• The starting line

Students find a partner. Teachers give each pair a starting line for a short scene and two characters: e.g. 'I need to talk to you': a teacher and student; two good friends; doctor and patient etc. Students need to show understanding of how a sentence can have different meaning depending on the context in which it is said.

• 'What are you doing?' game

Students stand in a circle. One person enters the circle and mimes something; e.g. sweeping the floor, feeding the cat, eating breakfast. Another person enters and asks, 'What are you doing?' The person in the circle answers with something different from what they are miming; e.g. if they are sweeping, they might answer, 'I'm feeding the cat'. The person who asked then stays in the circle and performs that action. The next person enters and the game continues. Teachers could allow the students to use a prop such as a ruler, which can help them to think of things – the ruler could become a tennis racquet, a broom, a pogo stick etc. This is a good game for quick thinking and gets the class members talking to each other.

• Mimes

Mimes are always an effective way to encourage nonverbal communication. Students can communicate anything from an emotion to a conflict scene.

• 'It's not me!' game

Students form groups of 5 – 10. The teacher secretly chooses one person to be an alien. The students then have to decide who the alien is by asking each other 'Is it you?' Everyone except the alien must tell the truth. The students must decide who is truthful and band together until one person is left on his/her own. We then find out the truth! This is lots of fun and gets the students working together and having to communicate honesty. Some students get really passionate about being believed. Others work out that it's fun to pretend to be the alien and fool everyone!!

Class count-up!

• This game takes practice and is a good way to emphasise the importance of listening to others. The class sits quietly facing the front. They are not allowed to turn and point to others or use body language such as facial expressions to indicate whose turn it is next. The teacher points to one student. That student says the number 'one'. The class must then continue counting until the number of students is reached (for example, if there are 26 students in the class they must get to 26).

Rules:
• Students can count only once per game.
• If a number is said twice, the game ends.
• If two or more students speak at the same time, the game ends.

You will find that the students begin to listen carefully and try to predict who will go next. Each day the class may get to a higher number. It can take weeks for the students to finish the game without breaking a rule. If they do this, there is jubilation all round and the class feels quite triumphant!

Communication and feelings – 'I' statements

Activity objective

- Completes 'I' statements to respond to a specific situation.

Curriculum links

England	PSHE	• 4c develop skills to be effective in relationships
Northern Ireland	PD	• know when it is important to express their feelings to others and how to do this in a positive way
Republic of Ireland	SPHE	• explore and practise how to handle conflict without being aggressive
Scotland	Health	• demonstrate responsible strategies to deal with a range of situations and emotions in a relationship
Wales	PSE	• listen carefully/question/respond to others

Teacher information

Being able to communicate effectively enables students to feel that they are getting their point across. One way to do this without being aggressive is to be assertive and use 'I' statements.

'I' statements are likely to be effective because they cannot be disputed. Children can begin sentences with 'I feel ...', or 'I don't like the way ...', so they cannot be argued with because it is how they are feeling! Also, by expressing how he/she is feeling, the student is not making any judgments about the person being disagreed with (so that person needn't become defensive!).

Three points to remember when being assertive and using 'I' statements are:

- Begin the sentence with 'I'.
- State how you feel.
- State the specific behaviour you don't like.

Students don't have to stick strictly to a formula as long as the basic structure is kept; for example, 'I'm starting to get angry', 'I don't like being called names' and 'I didn't realise this was so important to you. Can we work this out?'

Teaching problem-solving strategies through discussion and role-playing will assist students to learn and develop skills for positive social behaviours and relationships. 'I' statements are a good example of this. It is also important that the students making the 'I' statement have the body language to match.

Discussion points

- 'I' statements are a way of expressing your feelings. Why could 'I don't like the way you talk to me' be more effective than 'You always say horrible things to me. You have to stop!'?
- Allow the students the opportunity to share their responses.
- Role-play a conversation or argument that is full of 'you' statements. Ask the class to help change the dialogue to 'I' statements.

Additional notes

'I' statements

One way to get your point across to another person, without making the situation worse, is to be assertive. Being assertive allows you to state your views honestly and shows the other person that you respect yourself and them equally. Beginning a sentence with 'I' rather than 'you' (an 'I' statement) is a good way to communicate assertively. For example;

A takes B's pencil case and starts rummaging through it without asking.
B : You always touch my things without asking!
A: No I don't! (This conversation could keep going back and forth and may even lead to an argument.)

A takes B's pencil case and starts rummaging through it without asking.
B : I don't like it when you touch my things without asking.
 (B will hopefully respond with an apology.)

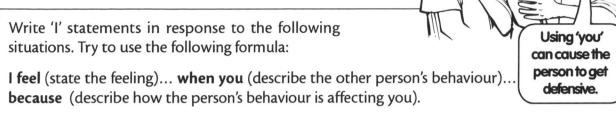

① Write 'I' statements in response to the following situations. Try to use the following formula:

I feel (state the feeling)… **when you** (describe the other person's behaviour)… **because** (describe how the person's behaviour is affecting you).

> Using 'you' can cause the person to get defensive.

(a) A boy in your class makes fun of you during PE because you keep missing the ball.

_____

(b) A boy in the class above you is always asking you about what your dad does for a living in front of everyone else because he wants them to laugh at you.

_____

(c) A girl in your class always announces to everyone when you bring something new to school. _____

(d) A boy in your class asks if you have a 'life' because you always do more homework than is required. _____

② Write an 'I' statement to respond to each of these statements.

(a) A: You're such a know-it-all! I think you've swallowed an encyclopaedia!

B: _____

(b) A: Why do you always get to go out of the class with Mrs Poncini? Don't you know how to read?

B: _____

(c) A: Did you fall in front of the lawn mower? That haircut's a nightmare!

B: _____

Now write your own.

(d) A: _____

B: _____

Communication and feelings – What makes you angry?

Activity objectives

- Identifies what makes him/her angry.
- Orders anger management strategies by personal preference.
- Describes and analyses an incident when he/she was angry.

Curriculum links

England	PSHE	• 4d realise the nature and consequences of aggressive behaviours
Northern Ireland	PD	• know how to recognise, manage and express their feelings and emotions
Republic of Ireland	SPHE	• discuss and practise how to express and cope with various feelings in an appropriate manner
Scotland	PSD	• begin to recognise a range of emotions and how they deal with them
Wales	PSE	• know and understand the range of their own and others' feelings and emotions

Teacher information

Most students will become angry at school for these reasons:
- conflict – verbal or physical,
- rejection – not being allowed to play with their friends etc.,
- being asked or made to do things they don't want to do,
- having their property or space invaded.

It is important for teachers to create an atmosphere in their classrooms that allows students to express and manage angry feelings. This can be done by ensuring that all rules are clear, fair and consistent; adopting anger management strategies for certain students (for example, a student is allowed to stand outside the classroom when he/she feels as though he/she is about to explode); good communication; and modelling positive anger management strategies.

As a teacher, help your students to deal with anger in a socially acceptable way. Unacceptable ways of expressing anger include hitting and pushing, sulking and crying excessively, or constantly looking for comfort solutions from a teacher or adult.

Ways to control anger include:
- taking a deep breath,
- counting to 10,
- getting away from the situation or person making you angry,
- trying to relax your body,
- exercising – going for a big run or bouncing a ball etc.,
- trying to stay calm,
- thinking and choosing the best way to react,
- telling yourself you are all right,
- talking about how you feel.

Discussion points

- Is it all right to be angry? What things shouldn't you do when you are angry?
- Is it all right to hurt someone else's feelings when you are angry?
- What signs let us know that we are about to get angry? (Discuss body language etc.)
- Discuss what can happen to adults (and children) who are unable to control their anger. Sometimes, people do illegal or harmful things to property and others when they are angry. Explain the importance of learning to control your anger when you are young.
- What could you do to help control the angry feelings you have? What do you do already?
- Ask the students to share the incidents that have made them angry with the class. Discuss their reactions.
- Role-play a situation where anger is building up.
- It isn't wrong to get angry but it is wrong to get angry and take it out on others.
- Think about things you have said and done to others when you have been angry. Have their feelings been hurt? Have they been physically hurt? After an incident such as this, we normally calm down and feel regret. Have you ever done something to another person that you now regret? Did you apologise?
- Ask the students to share their strategies for anger management. Discuss which techniques are appropriate for the classroom, the playground, at home etc.
- How can we help students who are learning to control their anger? (By not provoking them or 'cheering them on' when they get angry.)

What makes you angry?

We can't always avoid the people or things that make us angry but we can learn to control our anger. Anger is a natural emotion—it is part of life. It is okay to be angry but it is not okay to hurt anyone or damage someone's property because you are angry.

1 What (or who) makes you angry?
Write a list of things that make you angry.

I get ANGRY when...

Don't name names! For example, rather than saying, 'I get angry when Adam uses my cricket bat without asking', you could say, 'I get angry when people use my cricket bat without asking'.

2 There are many ways to deal with anger. Add some techniques to the list below and order them from 1 to 14 showing which you would use (1 being the way you control your anger the most and 14 the least).

Trying to relax your body		Keeping a journal and writing things down	
Counting to 10		Taking a deep breath	
Punching a pillow		Exercising (running around the playground)	
Telling yourself 'I'm okay, I'm all right'		Getting away from the thing/person that is making you angry	
Talking to someone		Telling the person why you are angry	

3 Write about a time when you were really angry.

_____

_____

_____

(a) Do you think you had control of your anger?

 Yes No

(b) Suggest ways you could have better controlled your anger.

Communication and feelings – Human rights

Activity objectives

- Devises a list of human rights.
- Analyses an example of a conflict.
- Describes own experience of a conflict where human rights were violated.

Curriculum links

England	PSHE	• 2e reflect on issues, using imagination to understand other people's experiences
Northern Ireland	PD	• know ways in which conflict and suffering can be caused by words/gestures/symbols/actions
Republic of Ireland	SPHE	• discuss how conflict can arise with different people and in different situations
Scotland	PSD	• discuss more than one strategy for coping with or tackling problems
Wales	PSE	• understand the situations which produce conflict

Teacher information

The international global community has decided on basic human rights, which are set forth as the General Declaration of Human Rights. The list contains rights such as:

- Right to human dignity
- Right to privacy
- Right to private property
- Equality before the law
- Freedom of movement
- Freedom of thought, conscience and religion
- Right to education
- Right to personal freedom.

This list has been formulated in an effort to ensure countries and their people support the basic rights and freedom of all.

Students have the right to feel safe when they come to school. They also have the right to be treated with respect and kindness; express their feelings and opinions; and work and play in an environment that has consistent, fair rules.

If students have difficulty describing a conflict they have been involved in where their rights may have been violated, ask the questions:

- Has anyone ever taken or touched your personal property?
- Has anyone ever stopped you from going anywhere?
- Has anyone ever hit or hurt you for no reason?
- Has anyone ever abused or ostracised you because of your ethnicity, religion or lifestyle?

Discussion points

- Discuss the rights listed on the worksheet. In what countries might these rights not be upheld? Why might this be?
- Discuss that everybody has the right to feel safe and that they deserve not to be bullied. In small groups, construct a list of rights for the classroom. What kinds of things may interfere with these rights? (Remember to stress that names of particular students should not be mentioned in whole-class discussions.)
- Let the students share their ideas with the rest of the class. Choose a few 'rights' to copy onto the board. Discuss with the class if there is anything or anyone who may interfere with these rights.
- Allow students the opportunity to share their 'classroom rights' with the class if they wish to. Find the answers common to each group.
- How can these rights be adopted into the classroom? What changes will need to be made to address the problems?

Additional activity

In small groups, develop a list of rights you feel should be upheld in your classroom. These might include things such as the right to be listened to, the right to change your mind, and the right to be treated with respect.

Human rights

1 (a) *Complete the sentences and decide if you deserve that right some of the time or always.*

☐ • Because I am a human being, I have the right to... _____

_____ sometimes/always

☐ • Because I am a human being, I have the right to... _____

_____ sometimes/always

☐ • Because I am a human being, I have the right to... _____

_____ sometimes/always

☐ • Because I am a human being, I have the right to... _____

_____ sometimes/always

(b) *Discuss each of the 'rights' you have chosen with other class members. Decide if it is a basic human right (R) or a human want (W) or wish. Write your decision in the boxes on the left.*

> Conflict can often lead to the violation of human rights.

2 (a) Read this example of how a team's rights were abused.

> *The year 6 football team from Oval Primary School won a competition to travel to Spain and play against a team from Barcelona. They walked around the city in their team shirts talking excitedly about the upcoming match. A group of teenagers nearby, in Spanish football shirts, began laughing and pointing at the team. They copied their language and pretended to play football really badly with each other, falling over and missing an imaginary ball. The team from Oval School started to yell at the teenagers and a heated argument erupted.*

(b) What rights do you think have been violated? _____

_____

_____

_____

3 Have you ever been involved in a conflict where you felt that your human rights were violated? Write about your experience below. (If you have not, write about an example of a conflict you have witnessed where rights were abused.)

Communication and feelings - Empathy

Activity objectives

- Considers the meaning of the word 'empathy'.
- Writes a diary entry from another person's point of view.

Curriculum links

England	PSHE	• 4a care about other people's feelings and to try to see things from their points of view
Northern Ireland	PD	• recognise and be sensitive to the feelings of others
Republic of Ireland	SPHE	• practise and recognise the importance of care, consideration, courtesy and good manners when dealing with others
Scotland	PSD	• recognise a range of emotions and how they deal with them
Wales	PSE	• empathise with others' experiences and feelings

Teacher information

Some people are often quick to make fun of anything unfamiliar. Some students prefer to ridicule others rather than to empathise with them. This activity will help students to put themselves in the place of another person who is, possibly, less fortunate than themselves.

Note: Dictionaries are required for this lesson.

Volunteers can read their diary entries to the class or a small group. How many different interpretations were there of Reece's life? Were any positive?

Be sensitive to any students in the class who may have similar behaviours to Reece.

Discussion points

- What is the difference between sympathy and empathy? (Dictionaries required here.)
- Is it okay to 'feel sorry' for someone?
- Can you think of a time when you empathised with someone you knew or heard about?
- How do you feel when you watch or read about a news story (such as September 11 or the Bali Bombings)? Even though you may not be affected personally by an event, do you think about those who have been?

Additional activities

- In groups, students can discuss the meaning of the word 'empathy'. They can show their representation of the meaning by choosing one of the following:
  - Create a mask that displays the expression 'empathy'
  - Create a collage that shows 'empathy'
  - Draw 'empathy'
  - Write a poem about 'empathy'
  - Create a cartoon strip that shows someone being 'empathetic'

Empathy

1 Read the diary entry below.

Dear Diary
27 April 2003

I want to tell you about a boy in my class. His name is Reece. You might say that he is small for an eleven-year-old. Most days, Reece is about ten minutes late to class. Miss Pendleberry never seems to tell him off though. Reece has three younger brothers and sisters all at the school. I see him walk them to and from school every day. He carries the youngest one's bag (I think her name is Kizzi) and sometimes even carries her! She must get tired on the walk home. I don't think Reece's clothes get washed very often. He can have a stain that will be on his school jumper all week! Sometimes Reece falls asleep in class. Aimee will bump him to wake him up. The other kids often laugh and call out things like 'sleepy head' and 'wake up Reece!'. Today Jamie called Reece a 'loser'. Miss P took Jamie outside and spoke to him. I was standing by the book corner but I couldn't hear what she said. I gave Jamie a big glare when he walked back in.

I've never seen Reece's mum or dad. Not even at sports days or assemblies. I might sit with Reece at lunchtime tomorrow. I think he might need a friend to talk to. Will let you know!

Sasha :)

2 What kind of person do you think Sasha is? _____

_____

3 What kind of person do you think Jamie is? _____

_____

Sometimes, when we think someone is different from us, we make fun of those differences rather than trying to understand the person or considering his/her feelings. Showing empathy for others is a skill that we should all learn, especially as we get older.

4 Find the dictionary meaning for the word **empathy** and write it in your own words.

_____

_____

_____

5 Imagine that you are Reece and you are writing in your diary. Write a diary entry that tells us a little bit more about your life. If you need to, continue on the back of this sheet.

Dear Diary   27 April 2003

_____
_____
_____
_____
_____
_____
_____
_____
_____

Team building – What makes a good team?

Curriculum links

England	PSHE	• 4c develop skills to be effective in relationships
Northern Ireland	PD	• recognise how to support peers in a positive way
Republic of Ireland	SPHE	• practise ways of working together
Scotland	Health	• demonstrate personal and interpersonal skills
Wales	PSE	• work cooperatively to tackle problems

Teacher information

Students could describe teams they have belonged to; e.g. school, sport, at home, in the community, for competitions.

Some team-building activities are provided on page 33.

The qualities of a good team include:

Working towards a clear goal – the team clearly understands and works towards the goal that is to be achieved. Each team member is focused on the tasks allocated by the team. The team defines any targets that need to be achieved as it works towards the common goal.

Good communication – the team members listen to each other with respect and willingly share their ideas without domination. Through this, the team members develop a mutual trust. Logical decisions are made with the acceptance of all team members.

Consideration – the team members encourage and support each other's ideas, giving critical feedback. Any criticism is aimed at the idea, rather than the person who contributed the idea. This encourages a willingness for the team to take risks and create new ideas. Everyone has an important role in the team.

Discussion points

- What teams are you/have you been a member of?
- What personal qualities does a good team member have?
- What could an effective team achieve compared to an ineffective one?

Additional notes

What makes a good team?

Carly attends art classes after school. Her class recently took part in an art competition which required people to work in teams. Carly's teacher entered four teams from the class, each made up of six children.

To their delight, Carly's team—The Leonardos—won the competition! Her team received a judge's report along with a prize of fabulous art supplies. Part of the report is below.

'Make a Mask' Team Competition — Judge's Report

GOAL: Each team is to design and make a mask in two hours, using the basic household materials supplied. The team that makes the mask judged to be the most creative will win.

TEAM NAME: The Leonardos

COMMENTS

Teamwork

This team began by asking one member to clearly state the goal so all team members understood precisely what they were working towards. The discussion that followed demonstrated excellent communication. Every team member listened to and considered others' ideas without interrupting. In addition, no-one dominated the conversation. Although a few members were at first hesitant to share their ideas, they were supported and encouraged to contribute. Whenever any team member disagreed with someone's ideas, he/she made critical comments about the idea, not the person. Everyone in the team seemed willing to take risks in this atmosphere of trust.

Before the team began to make the mask, it had made logical decisions which all team members had accepted. During the making, everyone was focused on the tasks they had been allocated by the team. Before the finished mask was presented to the judges, the team came together to discuss if anything else could be added.

(1) List the qualities of a good team that are mentioned in this report.

Team building - Teamwork group/self-evaluation

Activity objectives

- Evaluates the effectiveness of a team he/she has been part of.
- Evaluates the effectiveness of himself/herself as a team member.

Curriculum links

England	PSHE	• 4c develop skills to be effective in relationships
Northern Ireland	PD	• recognise how to support peers in a positive way
Republic of Ireland	SPHE	• practise ways of working together
Scotland	Health	• demonstrate personal and interpersonal skills
Wales	PSE	• work cooperatively to tackle problems

Teacher information

These proformas are for use after students complete a team activity. This may include team games or group projects/activities in areas such as science, technology and drama.

For each proforma, the students are to read each statement and circle the number that best describes their feelings.

Discussion points

- How could you become a more effective team/team member?
- How much does a team rely on contributions from all its members?

Additional notes

Teamwork group evaluation

Members of team: _____

_____

Team's goal: _____

_____

_____

The team had a clear understanding of the goal.	Clear	1	2	3	4	5	Unclear
The team was focused on achieving the goal.	Focused	1	2	3	4	5	Unfocused
Everyone participated.	Everyone	1	2	3	4	5	No-one
We listened to each other and gave feedback.	Excellent	1	2	3	4	5	Poor
We made decisions everyone agreed to.	Always	1	2	3	4	5	Never
We discussed and dealt with any problems.	Dealt with	1	2	3	4	5	Avoided
Risk-taking and creative ideas were encouraged.	Encouraged	1	2	3	4	5	Discouraged

Comment on how well the goal was achieved by the team. _____

_____

_____

Teamwork self-evaluation

Members of team: _____

_____

Team's goal: _____

_____

I had a clear understanding of the goal.	Clear	1	2	3	4	5	Unclear
I was focused on achieving the goal.	Focused	1	2	3	4	5	Unfocused
I contributed some great ideas.	Always	1	2	3	4	5	Never
I listened to others and gave feedback.	Excellent	1	2	3	4	5	Poor
I took part in the team's decision-making.	Took part	1	2	3	4	5	Took no part
I was a supportive team member.	Supportive	1	2	3	4	5	Unsupportive
I felt comfortable to take risks.	Comfortable	1	2	3	4	5	Uncomfortable

Comment on what kind of team member you were. _____

_____

_____

Team building – Team building activities

Curriculum links

England	PSHE	• 4c develop skills to be effective in relationships
Northern Ireland	PD	• recognise how to support peers in a positive way
Republic of Ireland	SPHE	• practise ways of working together
Scotland	Health	• demonstrate personal and interpersonal skills
Wales	PSE	• work cooperatively to tackle problems

Teacher information

- Each of the team building activities on the following page can be given to a small group. Teachers should set a time limit for each activity.

- The activities foster team skills such as communication, negotiation, working towards a goal, problem-solving, allocating tasks, risk-taking and creative thinking.

- Before completing any activity, instruct the students that talking to their team members is vital to complete each task successfully. The whole team must also agree on each decision that is made before it is carried out.

- Team numbers are suggested for each activity, but may be changed if teachers feel it is necessary. The only exception to this is 'Knot a Problem' – eight people is the minimum required for this activity to work successfully.

- As well as the materials listed below, each group will require paper and pencils to write ideas and/or plans for 'Puppet Challenge' and 'Advertising Agony'.

- Teachers may like to have each team present its creations/ideas to the class in the case of 'Puppet Challenge' and 'Advertising Agony'. 'Machines' must be presented to the class.

- A class discussion and student evaluation should follow the completion of each activity.

Discussion points

- What problems did your team encounter? How did you solve them?

- Were you happy with your team's work? Why/ Why not?

Additional information for each activity

Machines

– Teachers will need to discuss the types of machines that could be created for this activity; e.g. lawnmowers, juicers, bicycles, robots. Depending on the class's ability, teachers could even ask students to make imaginary machines; e.g. homework/dog grooming machines.

– Encourage students to choose sound effects and movements that make it easy for the audience to identify what is happening. Teachers may like for each team to announce the title of its machine before it presents it or may ask the class to guess after each presentation.

Puppet Challenge

– Each group will need a range of materials to choose from, including string, small pieces of wood, hole punches, material scraps, cardboard tubes, sticky tape, glue, lolly sticks, plastic spoons, pencils, felt-tip pens, colour paper scraps, staplers, aluminium foil, cotton reels, rubber gloves, wool, ribbons etc.

– Any sort of puppets may be made, including marionettes, glove or finger puppets. Depending on the class's ability, teachers could suggest some styles of puppets that could be made before the students begin the activity.

Advertising Agony

– Encourage students to read the problem carefully before they begin work. Teachers may suggest that teams nominate one person to read the problem aloud.

– Teams may devise ways to stop the flyers from being thrown away or may come up with some new low-budget advertising ideas.

Knot a Problem

– Do not attempt this activity on a hot day!

– When the circles are formed, some students may be facing outwards. Sometimes two circles will be formed.

Machines

Group of 6

Make a machine with your group, with each person being an important piece of the machinery. Add appropriate sound effects.

Begin by deciding what machine you will make and what each person will do.

When you present your machine to the class, show it starting up and slowly gathering speed, until it is working at its maximum speed.

The audience must be clear about what your machine is doing at all times.

Puppet Challenge

Group of 4

From the materials supplied, make a pair of puppets that will be appealing for four– to five–year-old children. The two puppets must look like they are part of a set (e.g. boy and girl; farmer and cow).

The puppets must be:

• safe for children

• able to be moved easily

• appealing to look at.

Advertising Agony

Group of 4 – 5

You are the owners of a new children's bookshop. You are competing against a large chain bookshop that is nearby, so you need to advertise.

Unfortunately, you do not have enough money for newspaper, radio or television advertisements, so you have been handing out flyers in the shopping centre.

However, people in the community have started to complain that your flyers are littering the streets—most people are throwing them away.

What can you do? You do not want to cause a litter problem, but you still need to advertise.

Knot a Problem

Group of 8

Stand in a circle with your group. Each person needs to reach across the circle and grab hold of two other hands. The hands each person grabs must belong to two different people.

Without letting go, the team must untangle the knot to make a circle. You will need to keep talking to each other to achieve this.

Conflict resolution skills – Steps for resolving a conflict

Teacher information

Conflict is an occurrence in every school, workplace and home. In schools, it is often the case that students faced with opposing viewpoints will go to a teacher to sort out the problem and make the final decision. Conflict resolution is a process that directs the responsibility for solving a conflict to the students. Students learn to express their point of view, voice their interests and find mutually acceptable solutions.

Conflict resolution steps are to be used, if possible, *before* conflicts reach a physical/violent stage. Students should be encouraged to use discussion to resolve minor conflicts such as name-calling, rumours, taking property without asking, teasing and invading personal space.

To resolve a conflict situation, students should feel comfortable enough to express their feelings, listen to others without feeling threatened and negotiate a solution that suits both parties.

The first priority is to establish a cooperative classroom and school environment where the rules, rights and responsibilities are clearly stated, and where students feel able to say what they feel. Students should be aware of class and school rules and their rights and responsibilities.

Schools that have implemented the conflict resolution programme are reporting that conflicts are being handled more quickly, physical fighting is declining and more caring behaviour is being noticed.

The steps on page 35 are one format for aiding students in resolving conflicts. The students may feel more ownership if they were to make up a class set of steps of their own. (See Appendix 1 on page 70 for a conflict resolution template.) Students may wish to practise saying the exact words to help remember them and to be able to bring them to mind quickly in a heated situation.

Students may decide on a format in simple words of their own such as the alternative below:

- What's the problem?
- _ What are the best ways to fix the problem?
- Choose the best option.
- Agree on the best solution and do it!

Teachers may wish to give each student a copy of the steps as a quick reference, or enlarge them and display them in the room for everyone to see.

Discussion points

- Discuss how students usually solve minor conflicts.
- Is there more than one good way to solve a conflict?
- What is the value of discussion in solving conflict?
- Discuss how compromise may be needed to resolve a conflict.

Steps for resolving a conflict

1

Stop and cool off.

2

Define the problem.
(Use 'I' statements.)

- Tell the other person what happened.
- Tell the other person how you feel.

3

Brainstorm solutions.

4

Choose a solution that is fair to both of you.
(Compromise is the key!)

5

Make a plan.

Decide how you will put it into action.

6

Agree to the plan.

- A handshake is a good way to show that you agree.

Conflict resolution skills – Conflict resolution

- Transforms a conversation so it follows the conflict resolution steps.

Curriculum links

England	PSHE	• 2f resolve differences by looking at alternatives, making decisions and explaining choices
Northern Ireland	PD	• know ways in which conflict and suffering can be caused by words/gestures/symbols/actions and ways in which conflicts can be avoided/lessened/resolved
Republic of Ireland	SPHE	• discuss how conflict can arise with different people and in different situations
		• identify and discuss various responses to conflict situations
Scotland	PSD	• discuss more than one strategy for coping with or tackling problems
Wales	PSE	• understand the situations which produce conflict
		• develop strategies to resolve conflict

Teacher information

Students can work in pairs to complete this activity. Depending on the noise level, students can perform their scripts as they create them. This should improve the authenticity of the scripts.

Ask volunteers to read their scripts to the class. As the students read, use the conflict resolution steps (page 35) to check off as each step is followed. Teachers may wish to give each student a copy of the steps as a quick reference, or enlarge them and display them in the room for everyone to see.

Discuss the similarities and differences among each of the scripts read.

Discussion points

- Discuss with the class reasons why it may be difficult to remember the steps when involved in a conflict.
- Ask the students if they have ever been involved in a similar conflict. What was the outcome?
- Discuss each step individually. Which are easier than others?
- Why is it important that the outcome must be agreed upon by both parties?
- Discuss how difficult/easy it will be for Maddy and Jason to follow through on the plans agreed on by the students.

Additional notes

Maddy and Jason are having a disagreement. They have not learnt about conflict resolution so some of the things they are saying are taking them further away from reaching a solution.

Complete their discussion using the Conflict Resolution steps. Remember that both parties need to agree on a solution. Compromise, on both sides, may be required to reach an agreement.

Remember
1. Stop and cool off.
2. Define the problem. (Use 'I' statements.)
   • Tell the other person what happened
   • Tell the other person how you feel
3. Brainstorm solutions.
4. Choose a solution that is fair to both of you. (Compromise is the key!)
5. Make a plan. Decide how you will put it into action.
6. Agree to the plan.

Maddy : You boys play football on the field every day! You are always hitting us with the ball or running into us while we are trying to talk. You don't even say sorry!

Jason: Talk! You girls don't talk. You sing and dance and prance around being stupid. Football is serious. We need as much of the oval as we can and we've got to practise 'cause the season's starting soon.

Maddy: _____

_____

Jason: _____

_____

_____

_____

_____

_____

_____

_____

**Try to see the situation from the other person's point of view.
If people can sense you're considering their feelings then they may be happier to compromise.**

Conflict resolution skills – Conflict role-plays

Activity objective

- Uses role-play to explore conflict situations.

Curriculum links

England	PSHE	• 2f resolve differences by looking at alternatives, making decisions and explaining choices
Northern Ireland	PD	• know ways in which conflict and suffering can be caused by words/gestures/symbols/actions and ways in which conflicts can be avoided/lessened/resolved
Republic of Ireland	SPHE	• discuss how conflict can arise with different people and in different situations
		• identify and discuss various responses to conflict situations
Scotland	PSD	• discuss more than one strategy for coping with or tackling problems
Wales	PSE	• understand the situations which produce conflict
		• develop strategies to resolve conflict

Teacher information

The role-play cards on the following page should be cut out and given to pairs of students. The students must role-play the conflict they think will be caused by each situation. Teachers may like the students to choose a situation and perform it for the class, or may like the students to try out each role-play over several weeks, perhaps performing them for another pair.

Teachers can instruct the students to resolve the conflict, or leave it up to the students to decide how they end the role-plays. However, teachers should encourage students not to make the role-plays screaming matches. The arguments used must be well-structured.

Discussion should follow the performances of the role-plays. This could include looking at reasons for the conflict starting, how each character dealt with it, what factors escalated the conflict etc.

Encourage the students to use clear speech and gesture to show how the characters are feeling.

Discussion points

- Do you think the characters in this role-play found a fair solution to their problem?
- What were A's (or B's) reasons for beginning the conflict?
- How well did the characters in this role-play deal with the conflict?
- Did the characters in this role-play use negotiation or problem-solving skills to help solve their conflict?

Additional notes

A and B are brothers/sisters.

A angrily accuses B of breaking his/her favourite CD. B remembers accidentally knocking over a pile of CDs the other day, but he/she does not feel it was his/her fault, because A left them on the floor.

A and B are shoppers.

A and B both reach a bargain table at the same time and pick up either end of the same item. It is something A and B both desperately want, and it is the last one left. They start to argue over who should get it.

A and B are flatmates.

A has just baked a birthday cake for a friend and left it on the bench to cool. Without realising this, B lets in the dog and it bounds straight to the bench and eats the cake. B has to tell A what has happened.

A and B are in the same class at school.

A is sick of being bullied by B. Every time B walks past A's desk, he/she knocks everything off, then walks away laughing. A decides to retaliate.

A and B are friends.

A is having problems with an English project. B is very good at English, so A asks B for some help. B refuses. A is annoyed, because he/she has helped B with his/her maths homework a number of times.

A and B are neighbours.

A has just bought a puppy, which is driving B mad. It barks constantly and runs into B's backyard through a hole in the fence between A and B's houses. When the puppy digs up B's garden, B decides he/she has had enough, and goes to see A.

A and B are brothers/sisters who share a room.

A has settled down to read quietly. At the same time, B walks in to do his/her trumpet practice. A and B start to argue about who should leave.

A and B are friends.

A has been told that B is spreading untrue rumours about him/her, so he/she has retaliated by spreading some rumours about B. B has just heard the rumours, and angrily comes to confront A.

A is a shopper, B is a shop assistant.

A is shopping in a department store. He/She has just walked past a display of vases. A is surprised when B taps him/her on the shoulder and asks him/her to pay for the vase he/she just broke. A is sure that it was not him/her.

A and B are in the same class at school.

A and B have been asked to work on painting a mural together. A hates B's ideas and B hates A's ideas. Their teacher tells them they cannot choose new partners. Both A and B want to get a good mark for their work.

Take care not to stir up the other person's emotions even further!

Conflict resolution skills - Conflict resolution evaluation

Activity objectives

- Describes and analyses a conflict situation.
- Identifies goals to resolve future conflicts more effectively.

Curriculum links

England	PSHE	• 2f resolve differences by looking at alternatives, making decisions and explaining choices
Northern Ireland	PD	• know ways in which conflict and suffering can be caused by words/gestures/symbols/actions and ways in which conflicts can be avoided/lessened/resolved
Republic of Ireland	SPHE	• discuss how conflict can arise with different people and in different situations
		• identify and discuss various responses to conflict situations
Scotland	PSD	• discuss more than one strategy for coping with or tackling problems
Wales	PSE	• understand the situations which produce conflict
		• develop strategies to resolve conflict

Teacher information

As students begin to learn about conflict resolution, they will be attempting to break habits such as the two most common reactions to conflict—'flight' or 'fight'.

The conflict resolution steps can be reinforced by using the evaluation sheet on page 41. Initially, students may not complete any of the steps. As they become more familiar with the conflict resolution process, more of the evaluation sheet will be completed.

Ensure students complete Question 9. It is important that they consider what they could have done differently. File the sheets so that they can be brought out and discussed if a similar situation occurs.

Discussion points

- Why do you think an evaluation of a conflict situation is necessary? Isn't it better just to forget about it?

- Why may it be difficult to remember the conflict resolution steps when involved in a conflict?

- What happens to you physically when you are arguing with someone? (Temperature rises, flushed, clench fists, heart beats faster, sweat etc.)

Additional notes

Conflict Resolution

Prim-Ed Publishing www.prim-ed.com

Conflict resolution evaluation

Name: _____ Class: _____ Date: _____

(1) Where were you when the conflict began?

[ ]

(2) Who was involved in the conflict?

[ ]

(3) Who witnessed the conflict?

[ ]

Steps Completed
1. *Stop and cool off* ☐
2. *Define the problem*
   - *Use 'I' statements* ☐
   - *Tell the other person what happened* ☐
   - *Tell the other person how you feel* ☐
3. *Brainstorm solutions* ☐
4. *Choose a solution that is fair to both of you. (Compromise is the key!)* ☐
5. *Make a plan. Decide how you will put it into action.* ☐
6. *Agree to the plan.* ☐

(4) Describe what started the conflict. _____

_____

(5) Did you tell the other person what you think happened and how you were feeling? ⸙ **Yes** ⸙ **No** ⸙

Explain. _____

_____

(6) Did both parties brainstorm solutions to the problem? ⸙ **Yes** ⸙ **No** ⸙

Explain. _____

_____

(7) *(a) Did you choose a solution that both parties thought was fair?* ⸙ **Yes** ⸙ **No** ⸙

(b) What was the chosen solution?

[ ]

(8) Did both parties agree to the solution? ⸙ **Yes** ⸙ **No** ⸙

Did you make a plan?

⸙ **Yes** ⸙ **No** ⸙

Yes – Describe your plan. _____

No – What will you do next? _____

(9) What will you do if faced with a similar situation in the future?

_____

_____

(10) Signed _____

Negotiation – What is negotiation?

Activity objectives

- Understands the steps involved in negotiation.
- Uses role-play to show the negotiation process.

Curriculum links

England	PSHE	• 2f resolve differences by looking at alternatives, making decisions and explaining choices
Northern Ireland	PD	• know ways in which conflict and suffering can be caused by words/gestures/symbols/actions and ways in which conflicts can be avoided/lessened/resolved
Republic of Ireland	SPHE	• discuss how conflict can arise with different people and in different situations
		• identify and discuss various responses to conflict situations
Scotland	PSD	• discuss more than one strategy for coping with or tackling problems
Wales	PSE	• understand the situations which produce conflict
		• develop strategies to resolve conflict

Teacher information

Negotiation is a problem-solving process used to resolve conflict. The goal of negotiation is to create a solution that the conflicting parties agree to.

Before a negotiation meeting, the people involved should think carefully about what they will say. The parties then meet in a quiet, neutral place; e.g. a 'negotiating table' in a corner of the classroom. The conflict is identified and an agreement to resolve it is made.

Both parties then use 'I' statements to describe the problem from their point of view. After each person speaks, the other restates what he/she has heard to show he/she has understood. Solutions to the conflict are then brainstormed, and the best solution is agreed upon.

Effective negotiation relies on clear communication, problem-solving skills, showing respect and a focus on finding a 'win-win' solution.

The role-play described on the following page could be performed to the whole class or a small group.

Discussion points

- Which features do you think an effective negotiator has? Could anyone learn to be an effective negotiator?
- What would hinder a successful negotiation?
- Why is it important to use 'I' statements?

Additional notes

What is negotiation?

Negotiation is a process in which people in conflict meet to resolve their dispute.

- Before meeting, each person thinks about the conflict and what he/she wants.
- The two people meet. They identify the problem and agree to try to solve it.
- Both people take turns to explain the problem, using 'I' statements to explain their feelings. The listener restates what the other person has said to show he/she understands.
- Possible solutions are brainstormed.
- One solution is decided upon. Both agree to try it.

① Read this conflict scenario.

Robyn and Jamie are working on a school project called 'Make a Magazine'. They are constantly arguing. Robyn is enthusiastic and has some great ideas on which she doesn't want to compromise. She feels Jamie is not doing her fair share of work. She is worried about this because she wants to get a top mark. Jamie feels Robyn is too bossy and doesn't listen to her. This has made her lose interest in contributing. She wants the magazine to include her ideas as well as Robyn's.

② Answer the questions to show how Robyn and Jamie could use negotiation to solve their conflict.

(a) List Robyn's and Jamie's wants.

Robyn wants _____

_____

_____

Jamie wants _____

_____

_____

(b) Write a sentence to explain the conflict.

_____

_____

_____

_____

(c) Write one 'I' statement each person might use. After each, write how the other person might restate this to show she has listened.

Robyn: I _____

_____

Jamie: You _____

_____

Jamie: I _____

_____

Robyn: You _____

③ Brainstorm two possible solutions to the conflict. Highlight the best one.

1
2

④ Find a partner. Use your answers to role-play Robyn and Jamie's negotiation. You can change the characters to boys if you need to. End your role-play with the characters agreeing to the chosen solution.

Negotiation – Discussing needs

Teacher information

Stating wants and needs is an important part of the negotiation process. Fair solutions to conflict can only be negotiated if both people understand what the other wants or needs.

When describing wants and needs, students should be encouraged to speak calmly and give reasons. When listening to someone else, they should demonstrate active listening through positive feedback and eye contact.

Students will need to work with a partner for the activity on the following page. Before the activity begins, each pair will need to decide who will play 'A' and who will play 'B'. The scenarios below can then be cut out and distributed. Instruct the students to look only at their own piece of paper.

Discussion points

- What are the benefits of expressing your wants or needs calmly?
- Did you find it easy or difficult to listen to your partner's wants and needs? Explain.

A *You are doing your homework in the lounge room at home on a Sunday night. It must be handed in to your teacher tomorrow morning, or you will not be able to play sport, which you love. While you are doing your work, your brother/sister comes in the room, puts on a CD and turns up the volume. You can't concentrate. You tell your brother/sister to leave. He/She refuses.*

B *You have just finished doing your homework in your bedroom and you need time to relax. You decide to listen to some music. The best CD player is in the lounge room, so you wander out, put on your favourite CD and turn up the volume. Your brother/sister is writing something at the coffee table and tells you to leave. You refuse.*

Discussing needs

Find a partner to work with. Read the scenario you are given. Don't look at your partner's!

(1) Think about your wants and/or needs. (List them on the back if you choose.)

(2) Take turns to tell each other what you want or need. Afterwards, write what you heard your partner say in the space below. Take turns to read aloud what you wrote.

_____

_____

_____

Hear, don't just listen!

(3) How well did your partner listen to you? Highlight his/her level of understanding.

ON FIRE	HOT	WARM	COLD	ICE-FORMING

If you chose 'Warm', 'Cold' or 'Ice-forming', ask your partner to listen to you again. Make sure he/she clearly understands your wants or needs before you go any further!

(4) On your own, write how you think both sets of wants and needs could be met.

_____

_____

_____

_____

_____

_____

_____

_____

(5) Discuss your answers to Question 4 with your partner. Decide on the best solution.

_____

_____

_____

_____

_____

_____

_____

_____

(6) Answer these questions on your own.

(a) Why was it important to listen carefully to each other? _____

_____

_____

(b) Why is it important to try to meet both sets of wants and needs? _____

_____

_____

(c) Were you happy with the chosen solution? Why/Why not? _____

_____

Negotiation - Brainstorming solutions

Activity objectives

- Understands how solutions are brainstormed during negotiation.
- Writes a play script that demonstrates brainstorming during negotiation.

Curriculum links

England	PSHE	• 2f resolve differences by looking at alternatives, making decisions and explaining choices
Northern Ireland	PD	• know ways in which conflict and suffering can be caused by words/gestures/symbols/actions and ways in which conflicts can be avoided/lessened/resolved
Republic of Ireland	SPHE	• discuss how conflict can arise with different people and in different situations
		• identify and discuss various responses to conflict situations
Scotland	PSD	• discuss more than one strategy for coping with or tackling problems
Wales	PSE	• understand the situations which produce conflict
		• develop strategies to resolve conflict

Teacher information

When students brainstorm solutions during negotiation, they should be focused on the goal of the negotiation. Depending on the complexity of the problem, the ideas could also be recorded in case the negotiation process needs to be revisited. Students may like to add this step to their play scripts.

This activity will encourage students to think creatively about possible solutions to a conflict.

Students may perform their plays to the class or a small group. If they follow the sample play script, they will also need a third student to act as their narrator.

Discussion points

- Do you think it is necessary to write ideas that are brainstormed during a negotiation? Why/Why not?
- Do you think all brainstormed ideas should be considered? Why/Why not?

Additional notes

Brainstorming solutions

① Read the play script below.

Narrator: Nicholas and Zac sit next to each other in their art class. Nicholas is new to the school and does not have any art pencils or a paint set. Their teacher has asked Zac to share his pencils and paint with Nicholas for a few weeks, which he has agreed to. However, they are in conflict because Nicholas keeps using Zac's pencils and paint without asking. He also returns Zac's pencils with chewed ends. The teacher suggests they go to the negotiating table in their classroom to sort out the conflict. Nicholas and Zac identify the problem and discuss their feelings. They are now ready to negotiate ...

Nicholas: Okay, now we understand how we feel about the conflict, let's think of some solutions. Any ideas?

Zac: Yes. I would like you to ask me when you need to borrow something.

Nicholas: But what if you're working? I don't want to bother you all the time.

Zac: That's true.

Nicholas: How about if I asked you for three or four pencils at a time?

Zac: That would be better. I'm also prepared to put my paint set between our desks so you don't have to ask for that.

Nicholas: Yes, that sounds fair. (He pauses.) Now, you also said you're not happy with the way I return your pencils.

Zac: Yes, they're always chewed on the ends.

Nicholas: It's a habit I have. I don't even know I'm doing it.

Zac: (scrunching up forehead) My cousin had the same problem, and she stuck some masking tape on the top of her pencils. That seemed to work.

Nicholas: That might ruin your pencils. I have a rubber pencil top at home that I could put on them. That would be better.

Zac: That's great! Okay, so this is our solution. You are going to ask me for a few pencils at a time. I'll put my paint set in the middle of the desks so you can use that without asking. And you are going to use your pencil top so I won't have soggy pencils any more! Do you agree?

Nicholas: I agree. Let's try it next time we have art.

Zac and Nicholas shake hands.

Being able to find a solution to a problem is a vital skill.

② Use the play script to write your own negotiating play script on a separate sheet of paper to perform with a partner. Some ideas are below.

• Two sisters or two brothers are constantly in conflict about who gets to use the family computer.

• A parent and a child are in conflict because the parent is always having to remind the child to practise the piano.

• Two children in a sports team are constantly putting each other down about their skills.

Negotiation – Problem-solving

Activity objective

- Uses problem-solving steps to find a fair solution.

Curriculum links

England	PSHE	• 2f resolve differences by looking at alternatives, making decisions and explaining choices
Northern Ireland	PD	• know ways in which conflict and suffering can be caused by words/gestures/symbols/actions and ways in which conflicts can be avoided/lessened/resolved
Republic of Ireland	SPHE	• discuss how conflict can arise with different people and in different situations
		• identify and discuss various responses to conflict situations
Scotland	PSD	• discuss more than one strategy for coping with or tackling problems
Wales	PSE	• understand the situations which produce conflict
		• develop strategies to resolve conflict

Teacher information

Problem-solving is an important skill that can be used in a range of curriculum areas. The steps on the following page can be used to solve problems in various situations.

Discussion points

- In what other situations besides negotiation could you use problem-solving steps?
- Could you leave any of the problem-solving steps out? Why/Why not?

Additional notes

Problem-solving

Most problems can be solved by following these simple steps.

To be a successful negotiator, you have to be a good problem solver.

- **Define the problem**

  Write a simple sentence which explains the conflict.

- **Brainstorm possible solutions**

  Use everyone's ideas, even if the group doesn't agree with or like the idea. Keep going until you can't think of any more ideas. Stay focused on the problem.

- **Evaluate the ideas**

  Ask these questions about each idea: Is it unkind? Is it unfair? Is it dishonest? Think about each idea's consequences by asking questions like 'What would happen if...?', 'How would doing this make each person feel?'

- **Decide on a solution and carry it out**

  It can help to restate the problem before you make a decision. The solution you choose should be a 'win-win' one.

Remember, don't analyse ideas during the brainstorming part.

(1) Find a group of four people. Use the problem-solving steps to find a fair solution to this scenario. Use the space beneath the problem for your notes.

> Amir, Scott and Carl sit next to each other in class. Amir and Scott constantly talk to each other during lessons, and are often in trouble with the teacher. She usually blames Carl for talking as well, although Carl hardly ever talks when he shouldn't. He feels angry that he is being told off for something he is not doing. Amir and Scott do nothing to help him, however. Carl wants to do well at school, but he also wants to stay friends with Amir and Scott. Amir and Scott don't want Carl to say anything to the teacher because they like sitting next to each other, although their marks at school are not good.

Notes

Our chosen solution:

Negotiation – Problem-solving activities

Activity objective

- Solves problems using problem-solving steps.

Curriculum links

England	PSHE	• 2f resolve differences by looking at alternatives, making decisions and explaining choices
Northern Ireland	PD	• know ways in which conflict and suffering can be caused by words/gestures/symbols/actions and ways in which conflicts can be avoided/lessened/resolved
Republic of Ireland	SPHE	• discuss how conflict can arise with different people and in different situations
		• identify and discuss various responses to conflict situations
Scotland	PSD	• discuss more than one strategy for coping with or tackling problems
Wales	PSE	• understand the situations which produce conflict
		• develop strategies to resolve conflict

Teacher information

Students will need to be familiar with the problem-solving steps described on page 49 before completing this activity. The page may be provided for students to refer to if teachers feel it is necessary.

For all the problems on the following page, students will need to write their solutions on a separate sheet of paper. The solutions and the process they used could then be discussed with the class.

The individual problems could be given to pairs of less able/confident students.

Discussion points

- What were some of the solutions you brainstormed but decided not to use? Why did you decide against them?
- Are you completely happy with your chosen solution? Why/Why not?
- Do you think there is a clear answer to the problem?

Additional notes

Lost key (Individual)

Use problem-solving steps to solve this problem.

Because your parents are going to be working late, they have given you a key to your house so you can let yourself in after school. Last time this happened, you lost the key and your parents had to change the locks on the doors. You have promised to be careful this time. However, when you get home, you realise you have left the key in your classroom. You know the classroom will be open until 5.30 p.m. You could walk there, but it would be dark by the time you got home and you know your parents would not like you walking in the dark. None of your neighbours has a key, and you are not keen to ring your parents.

What do you do?

School newspaper (Pairs)

Use problem-solving steps to solve this problem.

You are the editors of the school newspaper. You coordinate a group of writers to write about the life of the school.

One day, one of the writers gives you an article about the children from your class. It is well-written and very funny, but some of the comments are mean and some children may be hurt by it. However, the article is so good, you think it will increase sales. The money you make from the newspaper is donated to charity.

You must have the newspaper ready in an hour and you haven't got anything else that can fill the space.

What do you do?

Money (Pairs)

Use problem-solving steps to solve this problem.

You are friends who are sick of hearing about how much money one of your classmates has. She boasts about it all the time and teases anyone who does not have rich parents—and that includes both of you.

One day, you find an envelope on the ground with some money in it. You overhear your rich classmate telling her friend she has lost the money her parents gave her for 'something important', but she says she doesn't really care because her family has so much money anyway, she can simply ask for more.

What do you do?

Bullies (Individual)

Use problem-solving steps to solve this problem.

You are part of a large group of friends at school. Lately, the 'leader' of your group has started to bully a new girl in the class and has asked everyone in your group to join in. This involves calling her names, teasing her and pushing her over.

You don't like this idea, but you still want to remain friends with the gang. Before you have a chance to decide what to do, the new girl finds you alone one day and pleads with you to help her. You know if you do, you are likely to become a target for bullying too.

What do you do?

Negotiation - Evaluating negotiation

Activity objective

- Evaluates a negotiation in which he/she has taken part.

Curriculum links

England	PSHE	• 2f resolve differences by looking at alternatives, making decisions and explaining choices
Northern Ireland	PD	• know ways in which conflict and suffering can be caused by words/gestures/symbols/actions and ways in which conflicts can be avoided/lessened/resolved
Republic of Ireland	SPHE	• discuss how conflict can arise with different people and in different situations
		• identify and discuss various responses to conflict situations
Scotland	PSD	• discuss more than one strategy for coping with or tackling problems
Wales	PSE	• understand the situations which produce conflict
		• develop strategies to resolve conflict

Teacher information

The following page can be given to students who have used negotiation to solve a conflict. Part 1 should be completed immediately after the negotiation. Part 2 should be completed after the students have had a chance to try out their chosen solution. This will vary according to the situation, but should be at least a few days afterwards.

Discussion points

- What did the evaluation sheet reveal about your negotiating skills?

Additional notes

Evaluating negotiation

Complete Part 1 immediately after your negotiation has taken place. Complete Part 2 after you have begun to try your chosen solution—perhaps a few days or a week later.

PART 1   Date _____

Name of children _____

Conflict _____

_____

Brainstormed ideas

Chosen solution _____

_____

I agree to this solution.   Signed _____   _____

As part of our negotiation…

*   we showed respect towards each other.   Yes ☐   No ☐

*   we communicated well.   Yes ☐   No ☐

*   the chosen solution was the best of our brainstormed ideas.   Yes ☐   No ☐

*   the chosen solution is clear and realistic for both of us.   Yes ☐   No ☐

PART 2   Date _____

Write how you both feel about the solution now. _____

_____

_____

If you feel the solution is not working, will you:

*   *give it more time?* ☐   *• improve the solution?* ☐

*   *go back to your list of brainstormed ideas?* ☐

Explain your decision. _____

_____

_____

Peer mediation – Peer mediation steps

Activity objective

- Reads and discusses peer mediation steps.

Curriculum links

England	PSHE	• 2f resolve differences by looking at alternatives, making decisions and explaining choices
Northern Ireland	PD	• know ways in which conflict and suffering can be caused by words/gestures/symbols/actions and ways in which conflicts can be avoided/lessened/resolved
Republic of Ireland	SPHE	• discuss how conflict can arise with different people and in different situations
		• identify and discuss various responses to conflict situations
Scotland	PSD	• discuss more than one strategy for coping with or tackling problems
Wales	PSE	• understand the situations which produce conflict
		• develop strategies to resolve conflict

Teacher information

Peer mediation uses discussion to resolve minor conflicts between two students with the help of a professionally trained student mediator. It is based on the belief that resolutions are best reached with the help of a neutral third party and that children are more honest with and more likely to listen to peers than adults when discussing conflict. Common conflicts peer mediators face include name-calling, rumours, taking property without asking, teasing and invading personal space.

Peer mediators are trained to attack the problem, rather than the people involved. They encourage the parties to treat each other with respect. During the discussion, each person is required to state the problem, describe his/her feelings and say how he/she is responsible for the problem. Possible solutions are then brainstormed, and a fair solution that suits both parties is reached. Solutions may require compromise from both parties.

A successful peer mediation programme can enhance communication and problem-solving skills, create a more comfortable school environment and encourage tolerance of others. It can also be empowering for students because they are assuming a greater responsibility for their own problems.

Peer mediation is still in its infancy in terms of widespread practice in the UK and Ireland, but it is popular in the USA and Australia.

Peer mediation should only be attempted in a school where staff and students have attended a training course. Details of courses in peer mediation can be found on the Internet. Try typing 'school mediation courses' into a search engine.

Discussion points

- Ask the students to discuss with a small group the advantages and disadvantage of mediators being their peers and not teachers. What do they think would be the ideal age of a mediator to help resolve their conflicts?

Additional notes

Peer mediation steps

1 Ask the people involved in the conflict if they want to resolve the problem.

2 Find a private place to hold the mediation.

3 Explain the rules:
- Agree to listen to each other's opinions.
- No interrupting, yelling or put-downs.
- Always tell the truth.

4 Ask each person to explain the problem and describe how it makes him/her feel.

5 Rephrase what he/she said to you in your own words.

6 All people brainstorm as many solutions as possible.

7 Discuss each solution.

8 Choose a solution.
- This might involve each person compromising a little.

9 Both parties agree to the solution
- Show agreement, such as with a handshake or by signing an agreement form.

Peer mediation – Peer mediation 1

Teacher information

Peer mediation uses discussion to resolve minor conflicts between two students with the help of a professionally trained student mediator. It is based on the belief that resolutions are best reached with the help of a neutral third party and that children are more honest with and more likely to listen to peers than adults when discussing conflict. Common conflicts peer mediators face include name-calling, rumours, taking property without asking, teasing and invading personal space.

Peer mediators are trained to attack the problem, rather than the people involved. They encourage the parties to treat each other with respect. During the discussion, each person is required to state the problem, describe his/her feelings and say how he/she is responsible for the problem. Possible solutions are then brainstormed, and a fair solution that suits both parties is reached. Solutions may require compromise from both parties.

A successful peer mediation programme can enhance communication and problem-solving skills, create a more comfortable school environment and encourage tolerance of others. It can also be empowering for students because they are assuming a greater responsibility for their own problems.

Peer mediation is still in its infancy in terms of widespread practice in the UK and Ireland, but it is popular in the USA and Australia.

Peer mediation should only be attempted in a school where staff and students have attended a training course. Details of courses in peer mediation can be found on the Internet. Try typing 'school mediation courses' into a search engine.

Discussion points

- Discuss conflicts that occur in the home. Who is the 'mediator' at home? Make a list and tally the students' responses. Are they surprised with the results?

Additional notes

Peer mediation – 1

If you have a disagreement or problem with someone else, you might need a third person to help you sort it out. This person is called a mediator. Mediators are trained to help two people solve a problem. They do not judge anyone's behaviour and should have no investment in the outcome of the conflict. A good mediator listens to both sides of the story without taking sides.

1 Read the peer mediation steps below.

1. Introduce yourself as a mediator and ask the people involved in the conflict if they want to resolve their problem.

2. Find a private place to hold the mediation.

3. Explain the rules—the two people should agree to listen to each other's opinions; they should not interrupt, yell or put each other down; they should always tell the truth.

4. Ask the first person to explain the problem and describe how it makes him/her feel. Encourage him/her to say how he/she is responsible for the problem. Rephrase what he/she said to you in your own words.

5. Ask the second person to explain the problem and describe how it makes him/her feel. Encourage him/her to say how he/she is responsible for the problem. Rephrase what he/she said to you in your own words.

6. All three people brainstorm as many solutions as possible.

7. Everyone discusses each solution. The mediator helps the two people decide if one is fair and sensible.

8. Everyone decides on a fair solution that makes both people happy. This might involve each person compromising or giving way a bit.

9. Both parties agree to the solution (show agreement, such as with a handshake or by signing an agreement form).

2 Do you think you have the qualities to be a good mediator? Answer these questions.

(a) Do you generally speak nicely to your peers? **Yes** **No**

(b) Do you like to help others? **Yes** **No**

(c) Does it make you unhappy to see things that just 'aren't fair'? **Yes** **No**

(d) Are you good at keeping secrets? **Yes** **No**

(e) Are you good at not taking sides when people are arguing? **Yes** **No**

(f) When someone is talking to you, can you listen without giving your opinion or telling your own similar stories? **Yes** **No**

(g) Can you be empathetic (putting yourself in someone else's shoes) when you hear a story? **Yes** **No**

(h) Would you be happy to give up some of your free time? **Yes** **No**

3 Do you think you would be a good mediator? Describe why or why not.

_____

_____

keep voice low   check that both parties understand what the other said   encourage 'I' statements

Peer mediation - Peer mediation 2

Activity objective

- Demonstrates knowledge of the peer mediation steps by writing a play script.

Curriculum links

England	PSHE	• 2f resolve differences by looking at alternatives, making decisions and explaining choices
Northern Ireland	PD	• know ways in which conflict and suffering can be caused by words/gestures/symbols/actions and ways in which conflicts can be avoided/lessened/resolved
Republic of Ireland	SPHE	• discuss how conflict can arise with different people and in different situations
		• identify and discuss various responses to conflict situations
Scotland	PSD	• discuss more than one strategy for coping with or tackling problems
Wales	PSE	• understand the situations which produce conflict
		• develop strategies to resolve conflict

Teacher information

Students need to be familiar with the peer mediation steps on page 55 before attempting this activity. This page may be provided for students to refer to if teachers feel it is necessary. To bring the task to life, ask two students to role-play the argument between the two younger students.

This activity will also work well for students working in small groups. Students can brainstorm possible solutions to the conflict and plan the play script together. The play can be written independently or in small groups.

Ask individual students or groups to share their plays with the class.

Discussion points

- After students have shared their play scripts with the class, discuss the different ways the conflict was resolved. Was it difficult brainstorming a solution that both students would be happy with?

- Discuss the benefits of mediation. Students may mention that, with mediation, the problem is usually resolved a short time after the conflict occurs. When conflicts are not resolved immediately, negative feelings can brew and thoughts of the next meeting with the person involved can lead to worry or anxiety.

Additional notes

Peer mediation – 2

You come home from basketball training and hear raised voices coming from the lounge. You remember that your younger brother invited a friend over to play.

Keep your voice quiet and controlled.

This is what you hear.

Riley (your brother):	Look! It's my Nintendo™. I'm playing it!
Jack:	But that's not fair! I want to have a go too. You've been hogging it for ages and I'm a guest!
Riley:	You can just wait! I'm at a good bit.
Jack:	I'm going to call my mum and get her to pick me up!
Riley:	Whatever!

Remember:
1. Ask
2. Set the rules
3. Person 1 describes the problem
4. Person 2 describes the problem
5. Brainstorm
6. Discuss solutions
7. Decide on a solution

You decide to put your peer mediation training into practice and speak to the boys. Write an 'ideal' dialogue between you and the boys. You will need to use the peer mediation steps and brainstorm a number of solutions that will appeal to both children.

Peer mediation - Peer mediation 3

Activity objectives

- Brainstorms possible solutions to conflict situations.
- Role-plays scenarios involving peer mediation.

Curriculum links

England	PSHE	• 2f resolve differences by looking at alternatives, making decisions and explaining choices
Northern Ireland	PD	• know ways in which conflict and suffering can be caused by words/gestures/symbols/actions and ways in which conflicts can be avoided/lessened/resolved
Republic of Ireland	SPHE	• discuss how conflict can arise with different people and in different situations
		• identify and discuss various responses to conflict situations
Scotland	PSD	• discuss more than one strategy for coping with or tackling problems
Wales	PSE	• understand the situations which produce conflict
		• develop strategies to resolve conflict

Teacher information

Organise the students into groups of three. Ask each group to read the scenarios and discuss possible solutions. Explain that it doesn't matter how silly or over-the-top their ideas may be as they could lead to a solution that all students agree on.

Students choose (or are allocated) one of the scenarios to role-play. The mediator will need to model the peer mediation steps described on page 57.

Allow time for the groups to rehearse their role-plays and then perform them for the class. Compare the groups who presented the same scenario. Were the outcomes similar? Why or why not?

Discussion points

After each scenario is read:

- What would you do in that situation?
- If you were a peer mediator, how would you approach each group of students? Why or why not? Was there a solution?
- Why do you think Jerome became agitated with Ahmed and Mohammed?

    (If there are any Muslim children in your class, you may like to ask them prior to the lesson if they would talk to the class about the celebration of Ramadan.)

Additional notes

Peer mediation – 3

① In groups of three, read each scenario listed below and brainstorm possible solutions. Record your brainstormed ideas in the boxes.

② Choose one scenario and create a role-play based on the problem. Take turns being the mediator.

(a) Danny and Reece had to go and collect the footballs from the PE cupboard and take them out to the basketball court. The boys ran to the cupboard and both reached for the bag of balls. Danny told Reece to take the cones but Reece shook his head saying that he wanted to carry the footballs outside. Just then, a Year 6 child walked past. She asked the boys if they needed some help to resolve the problem.

(b) Sara and Abbey were well known as being the best at drama in the school. They were always chosen to play the main parts in the end-of-year production. However, this year, the play only had one main part and Abbey had won the role. Since then, Sara hadn't spoken to Abbey. Mr English noticed that the girls' feuding was unsettling the class. He asked Eniola, a peer mediator, to speak to the girls.

(c) Reanna was very loud and liked to voice her opinions in class. Shaun was trying hard to show his teacher and parents that he could work hard at his class work without getting distracted as he wanted to join the debating club that met during school time. Whenever their teacher asked a question in class, Reanna yelled out her answer or opinion over the top of everyone else. Shaun had had enough so he went and told Reanna to 'shut up'.

(d) Ahmed and his brother Mohammed are celebrating the Ramadan festival and are fasting during all daylight hours for one month. During lunch, Jerome watches Ahmed and Mohammed sitting on the field not eating any lunch. He walks over to them and asks why they aren't eating. Their answer doesn't satisfy him so he keeps saying again and again, 'But if you're hungry, just eat!' Ahmed stands up and starts yelling at Jerome to go away. Simon has watched the conflict. He walks over to Ahmed and Jerome and asks if they would like to talk about it.

Peer mediation - Peer mediation evaluation

Activity objectives

- Describes and analyses a peer mediation situation.
- Identifies goals to make future peer mediation more effective.

Curriculum links

England	PSHE	• 2f resolve differences by looking at alternatives, making decisions and explaining choices
Northern Ireland	PD	• know ways in which conflict and suffering can be caused by words/gestures/symbols/actions and ways in which conflicts can be avoided/lessened/resolved
Republic of Ireland	SPHE	• discuss how conflict can arise with different people and in different situations
		• identify and discuss various responses to conflict situations
Scotland	PSD	• discuss more than one strategy for coping with or tackling problems
Wales	PSE	• understand the situations which produce conflict
		• develop strategies to resolve conflict

Teacher information

Not all students possess the personality to be an effective mediator. Choose the students to train in this process carefully. Once the students have assisted in their first peer mediation, sit with them individually and complete the proforma on page 63.

Devise goals for the next peer mediation and make a time (perhaps in a week) to meet with the students and identify if the set goals have been met.

Discussion points

- What are the qualities of a good mediator?
- Does everyone possess these qualities? Why not?
- What factors may contribute to making a peer mediation unsuccessful?
- List any 'troubleshooting' that may help a mediator transform a negative situation into a positive one.

Additional notes

Peer mediation – evaluation

Mediator: _____   Date of peer mediation: _____

1. How did you learn of the conflict situation that required a mediator?

   [ ]

   Steps Completed
   - Ask ☐
   - Set the rules ☐
   - Person 1 describes the problem ☐
   - Person 2 describes the problem ☐
   - Brainstorm ☐
   - Discuss solutions ☐
   - Decide on a solution ☐

2. How did you introduce yourself?

   [ ]

3. Did you explain the rules to the people involved? ⟨Yes⟩ ⟨No⟩
   What rules did you state?

   [ ]

   You weren't bossy, were you?

4. Describe how you helped both parties to explain their stories.

   [ ]

5. Did all parties cooperate in brainstorming a solution? ⟨Yes⟩ ⟨No⟩ Explain.

   [ ]

6. Did all parties agree to the chosen solution? ⟨Yes⟩ ⟨No⟩ Explain.

   [ ]

7. Do you feel that you assisted in a successful and effective peer mediation? ⟨Yes⟩ ⟨No⟩ Explain.

   [ ]

8. Choose three goals to aim at for your future peer mediations.   Achieved

   - _____   ___/___/___
   - _____   ___/___/___
   - _____   ___/___/___

Peace – Peaceful Island?

Activity objectives

- Gains an understanding that peace depends on action and communication.
- Suggests some ways peace can be created.

Curriculum links

England	PSHE	• 2d know there are different kinds of rights at home/in the community and that these can sometimes conflict with each other • 2f resolve differences by looking at alternatives, making decisions and explaining choices
Northern Ireland	PD	• know ways in which conflict and suffering can be caused by words/gestures/symbols/actions and ways in which conflicts can be avoided/lessened/resolved
Republic of Ireland	SPHE	• discuss how conflict can arise and be handled
Scotland	PSD	• discuss more than one strategy for coping with or tackling problems
Wales	PSE	• understand the situations which produce conflict and develop strategies to resolve conflict

Teacher information

Peace is often thought of as a passive state—a lack of war. But peace is a process which requires action to be started and sustained. Obstacles to peace include fear of the unknown or the unfamiliar.

Each student will need to choose a partner for this activity. Before the pairs begin the activity, they must decide who will be the chief of Jadda clan and who will be the chief of Pinka clan. As well as the activity sheet on the following page, each student will need a copy of the description of his/her clan below. It is important the student does not read his/her partner's description at any time. The success of the activity relies upon the students communicating with each other to achieve peace.

Discussion points

- Why do you think the clans in the activity fight with each other?
- Peace takes action and communication. Discuss.
- What do world leaders do to promote peace?
- What are some ways you could promote peace in your school or community?
- Discuss obstacles to peace, and how they could be overcome; e.g. different cultural values or beliefs.

Jadda Clan

Your clan lives on the east side of the island. The other clan is the Pinka clan, which lives on the west side. Every morning, your clan does a traditional dance, which involves the beating of drums. This seems to annoy the Pinka clan, although you are not sure why. You only eat fish and plant-life, including the wasta plant, which you believe has healing properties. You are unhappy that the Pinkas live on the west of the island, because 100 years ago your people used to live there, but were driven away by the Pinkas.

Your clan and the Pinkas use the same stream for drinking water, although there are also three freshwater lakes on the island. You would like the Pinkas to get their water elsewhere. You find their dress offensive, as they wear little clothing. The Pinkas also regularly swim in Ranji Lake, which is sacred to you. Your tribe finds this disrespectful.

Pinka Clan

Your clan lives on the west side of the island. The other clan is the Jadda clan, which lives on the east side. Every morning, your clan prays quietly, but is always interrupted by the Jaddas making a terrible noise. You think they do this just to annoy you. You dislike the fact that the Jaddas eat the wasta plant, which is sacred to you. You eat mostly fish, but feel that the Jaddas take too many.

Your clan and the Jaddas use the same stream for drinking water, although there are  also three freshwater lakes on the island. You would like the Jaddas to get their water elsewhere. Your clan often visits Ranji Lake, where you teach your children to swim. The Jaddas don't seem to like this, but you are not sure why.

Peaceful island?

Cobi is a small island inhabited by two clans. Unfortunately, it is not a peaceful place. The two clans often war with each other, due to their differences.

Imagine you and your partner have just become the new chiefs of the two clans. You would like to live in peace with each other. You both realise this will not just happen—it will take some action.

① Read the description of your tribe.
   NB – Do not read the description of your partner's clan.

② You and the other chief agree to meet to discuss how you can live in peace. Before you meet, answer these questions.

   (a) Why is peace important to you? _____

   _____

   (b) Describe your clan's major issues and any questions you would like to ask the other chief. Peace relies on communication, so make sure your questions seek to clarify anything about the other clan you are not sure of.

Major issues	Questions

③ Use your answers to help you discuss how to create peace with the other chief. You may also refer to the description of your clan to answer questions asked by the other chief, but don't read the whole description aloud!

   Make sure you create solutions both of you agree upon. Write notes about your ideas and final decisions in this space and report to the class.

Peace – What does peace mean to you?

Activity objective

- Considers the meaning of peace.

Curriculum links

England	PSHE	• 2e reflect on moral and social issues
Northern Ireland	PD	• express their views
Republic of Ireland	SPHE	• identify the behaviour that is important for harmony
		• explore how peace can be promoted
Scotland	PSD	• recognise a range of emotions
Wales	PSE	• know and understand the range of their own feelings and emotions

Teacher information

Peace is quite an obscure topic to discuss so this activity may be more effective if students work in small groups, allowing them to bounce ideas off each other. To begin the lesson, ask the students to name their favourite films. Listen to their suggestions and write any 'action' or 'violent' film titles on the board. Ask the class why they think these films are popular.

Ask the students what they think the opposite of peace is. If students answer with war, discuss how war is often portrayed in films as being exciting when it is actually violent and destructive.

Acrostic 'peace' poems can be presented on coloured card for display.

An acrostic poem is written using the first letters of a word. Acrostic poems may or may not contain rhyme. Students can use a dictionary and thesaurus to help them find words beginning with certain letters.

Discussion points

- What does it mean to live in peace?
- Do we live in peace today?
- How can we promote peace in our classroom, schools, homes and communities?
- What is a peacemaker? Have you ever had to 'make peace' between two people in conflict with each other. How did you succeed at making peace?

Additional activity

- Create a 'Book of Peace' for the classroom.
  Students can add:
  – descriptions of 'peace acts' they have performed or witnessed,
  – messages of peace for their friends,
  – ideas to promote peace in the classroom/school/play area.

① In your group, write words and phrases that describe what peace means to you.

PEACE

② Answer these questions and **give a reason** for each.

(a) What colour is peace?	*(b) What does peace sound like?*
(c) What does peace feel like?	*(d) What does peace look like?*

③ Complete the acrostic poem below by using the words and phrases you wrote above.

P _____

E _____

A _____

C _____

E _____

We can all do our bit in our little part of the world.

④ Think of one way you can help promote peace **today** in your:

(a) classroom

(b) school

(c) home

Tolerance – What is tolerance?

Activity objective

- Gains an understanding of the importance of tolerance.

Curriculum links

England	PSHE	• 4f know that similarities and differences between people arise from a number of factors
Northern Ireland	PD	• recognise and be sensitive to the feelings of others
Republic of Ireland	SPHE	• recognise and appreciate that each person is a unique individual
Scotland	PSD	• demonstrate respect and tolerance towards others
Wales	PSE	• respect others and value uniqueness

Teacher information

Teaching children tolerance is also teaching them not to hate. Teachers can teach tolerance most effectively by modelling tolerant behaviour in the classroom and playground. Ensure students are exposed to people, literature and images that are multicultural and teach them about other beliefs, ethnicity and lifestyles. As the students reach the end of primary school, they become more aware of the world around them and news stories. Ask the students to talk about any instances of prejudice and discrimination that they have heard about or witnessed.

Educating students to be tolerant will:

- promote the understanding and acceptance of individual differences,
- minimise generalisations and stereotyping,
- help students to understand and appreciate the differences among people,
- promote the need to counter prejudice and discrimination.

Discussion points

- Discuss definitions of tolerant, intolerant, tolerable, tolerate etc.
- Why is tolerance important? Does it mean you have to agree with other people's beliefs?
- Discuss the outcomes of intolerant behaviour in the community.
- What could be achieved through a more tolerant society?
- Brainstorm the names of famous people who have striven for peace through tolerance; e.g. Nelson Mandela.

Additional notes

What is tolerance?

1 Complete the chart with a partner. (Choose someone you don't normally spend time with.)

Question	Your response	Your partner's response
What is your favourite style of music?		
Do you believe in ghosts?		
What is something that makes you happy?		
What is your favourite room in your house and why?		
What is your most prized possession?		
What is your biggest fear?		
If you could go anywhere in the world, where would you go?		
What is your favourite food?		
Do you have a secret ambition? What is it?		
Name something that you consider to be beautiful.		
What is your definition of peace?		

2 *(a) Did you and your partner have many similar answers?* Yes No

(b) Imagine a world where people looked the same, spoke the same and liked and wanted the same things. What do you think it would be like?

_____

_____

(c) Being tolerant means being patient and fair towards people with opinions and customs different from our own.

Write a creative story about a group of children who learn the important lesson of being tolerant towards each other. On the back of this sheet, plan your story. Include characters, setting, plot, conflict and resolution.

Differences among us enrich our lives.

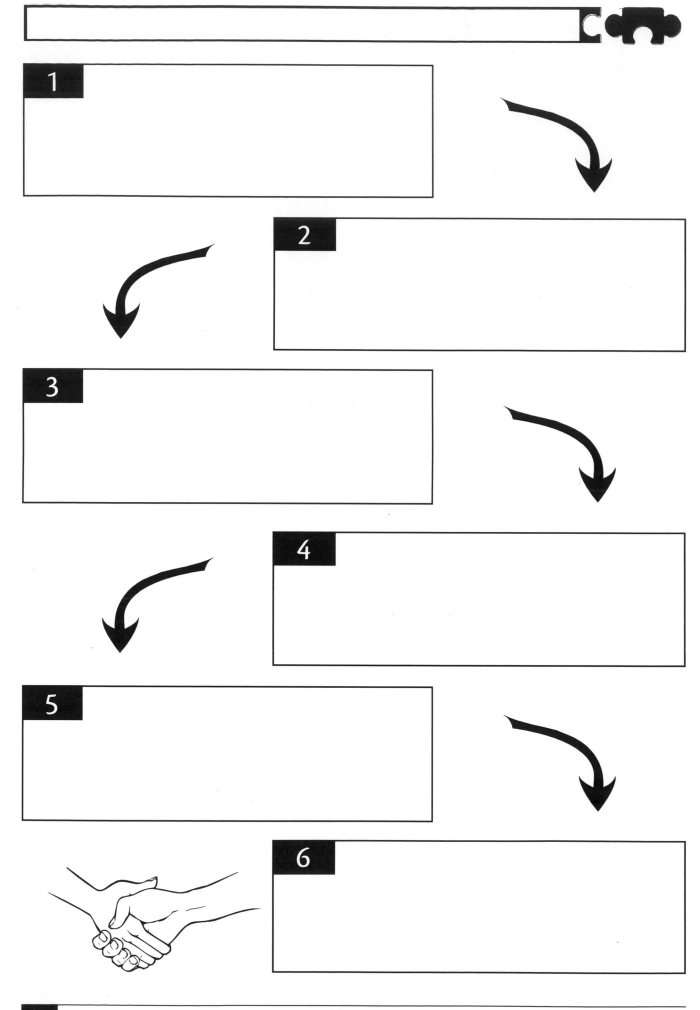

1

2

3

4

5

6